9FRONT
FREQUENTLY
QUESTIONED
ANSWERS

This book was typeset (`troff -ms -mpictures|lp -dstdout|ps2pdf`) in Lucida Sans
by the author, using a ThinkPad X61 Tablet running the 9front operating system.

Rendered: 2021-7-29

9FRONT
9front.org

ISBN-13: 978-1-300-34236-6

The study of this Book is forbidden. It is wise to destroy this copy after the first reading.

Whosoever disregards this does so at his own risk and peril. These are most dire.

Those who discuss the contents of this Book are to be shunned by all, as centres of pestilence.

All questions of the Law are to be decided only by appeal to my writings, each for himself.

There is no law beyond Do what thou wilt.

⑨ 9front System

ACHTUNG! 9front dash1 manual is written by and for 9front users.

Those who can do, those who can't write and those who can't write make ezines.
— Sape Mullender

ACHTUNG! Information provided by this document is UNOFFICIAL and may be outdated or just plain WRONG. Use your brain. NO REFUNDS.

_sl's info is incorrect.
— anth_x

ACHTUNG! 9front is absolutely and unalterably opposed to racism, sexism, homophobia, transphobia, nationalism, ethnocentrism, religious fundamentalism, and oppressive and coercive power structures of all kinds.

Nobody wants 2 take the weight – The responsibility
— Prince,
Avalanche

ACHTUNG! Don't read too much into what you find here.

Unless this publication states otherwise, masculine nouns and pronouns do not refer exclusively to men.
  FM34 60 COUNTERINTELLIGENCE

0 – Introduction to Plan 9

0.1 – What is Plan 9?

0.1.1 – Plan 9 is not UNIX

0.1.1.1 – Plan 9 is not plan9port

0.1.1.2 – Plan 9 is not Inferno

0.1.2 – Plan 9 is not a product

0.1.3 – Plan 9 is not for you

0.2 – Why Plan 9?

0.2.1 – What do people like about Plan 9?

0.2.1.1 – What do you use Plan 9 for?

0.2.2 – What do people hate about Plan 9?

0.2.2.1 – What is not in Plan 9

0.2.3 – Why did Plan 9's creators give up on Plan 9?

0.2.3.1 – Why did Plan 9's users give up on Plan 9?

0.2.3.2 – Why did CIA give up on Plan 9?

0.2.4 – What is the deal with Plan 9's weird license?

0.2.4.1 – Richard Stallman hates the Plan Nine license (circa 2000)

0.2.4.2 – Theo de Raadt hates the Plan 9 license (circa 2003)

0.2.4.3 – Everyone hates the Plan 9 license (circa 2014)

0.2.4.4 – PRAISE FOR 9FRONT'S BOLD ACTION RE: LICENSING

0.2.4.5 – Everyone loves the Plan 9 license (circa 2021)

0.3 – Further Reading

0.3.1 – Plan 9 papers

0.3.2 – Man pages

0.3.3 – Web pages

0.3.4 – Books

1 – Introduction to 9front

1.1 – What is 9front?

1.1.1 – Cirno

1.2 – On what systems does 9front run?

1.3 – Why might I want to use 9front?

1.3.0 – Why might I not want to use 9front?

1.3.0.1 – Why did 9front stop making fun of Nazis?

1.3.1 – New Features

1.3.1.1 – New Programs

1.3.1.2 – New Hardware Support

1.4 – Is 9front really free?

1.5 – How can I help support 9front?

1.6 – Who maintains 9front?

1.7 – When is the next release of 9front?

1.8 – What is included with 9front?

1.9 – Can I use 9front as a desktop system?

1.10 – Why is/isn't ProductX included?

1.11 – Fine, where can I get 9front?

1.11.1 – Mirrors

1.11.1.1 – 9front.iso

1.11.1.2 – Mercurial repository

2 – Getting to know 9front

2.1 – Web Pages

2.2 – Mailing Lists

2.2.1 – Mailing List Archives

2.2.2 – Other useful mailing lists

2.3 – Manual Pages

2.3.2 – How do I write my own manual page?

2.4 – Reporting Bugs

2.4.1 – Your bug report SUCKS

2.4.2 – How do I get more useful info for developers?

2.4.2.1 – Take a photo of the panic screen

2.4.2.2 – Make a stack trace of a crashed process

2.4.2.3 – Make a process snapshot

2.5 – Sending Fixes

2.5.1 – How do I write good patches?

2.5.2 – How do I send in my patches?

3 – Hardware

3.1 – Selecting Hardware

3.2 – Known Working Hardware

3.2.0 – Input Devices

3.2.0.1 – Mice

3.2.0.1.1 – IBM/Lenovo

3.2.0.2 – Keyboards

3.2.0.2.1 – IBM/Lenovo

3.2.0.2.2 – TEX Electronics

3.2.1 – Audio

3.2.2 – Graphics

3.2.2.1 – AGP

3.2.2.2 – Integrated

3.2.2.3 – PCI Express

3.2.3 – Networking

3.2.3.1 – Ethernet

3.2.3.1.1 – Integrated

3.2.3.1.2 – USB

3.2.3.1.3 – PCMCIA

3.2.3.2 – WiFi

3.2.3.2.1 – Bridge (external)

3.2.3.2.2 – Mini-PCI

3.2.3.2.3 – Mini-PCI Express

3.2.3.2.4 – PCI

3.2.3.2.5 – PCMCIA

3.2.4 – Tablet Digitizers

3.2.4.1 – Serial

3.2.4.1.1 – Integrated

3.2.4.2 – USB

3.2.4.2.1 – Integrated

3.2.4.2.2 – External

3.2.5 – Laptops

3.2.5.1 – Acer

3.2.5.2 – IBM/Lenovo

3.2.5.2.1 – ThinkPad

3.2.5.3 – Toshiba

3.2.5.3.1 – Satellite

3.2.6 – Desktops

3.2.6.1 – eMachines

3.2.6.2 – Igel

3.2.6.3 – Soekris

3.2.6.4 – IBM/Lenovo

3.2.6.4.1 – ThinkCentre

3.3 – Virtual Machines

3.3.1 – Qemu

3.3.1.1 – Installation

3.3.1.2 – Post-Installation Booting

3.3.1.2.1 – Multiboot

3.3.1.4 – Networking

3.3.1.4.1 – Linux VDE

3.3.1.4.2 – OpenBSD TAP

3.3.1.4.3 – Windows TAP

3.3.1.4.4 – Linux TAP

3.3.1.5 – Audio

3.3.1.6 – Graphics

3.3.2 – Virtualbox

3.3.2.1 – Ethernet

3.3.2.2 – Audio

3.3.2.3 – Graphics

3.3.2.4 – Known Working Versions

3.3.3 – Virtio

4 – 9front Installation Guide

4.1 – Pre-installation Checklist

4.2 – Creating bootable 9front install media

4.2.1 – ISO image

4.2.2 – USB drive

4.2.2.1 – Creating on Plan 9

4.2.2.2 – Creating on Linux

4.2.2.3 – Bootargs

4.3 – Performing a simple install

4.3.1 – boot

4.3.2 – bootargs

4.3.3 – user

4.3.4 – vgasize, monitor, mouseport

4.3.4.1 – Changing screen resolution

4.3.5 – inst/start

4.3.6 – configfs

4.3.6.1 – cwfs no-dump configuration

4.3.7 – partdisk

4.3.8 – prepdisk

4.3.9 – mountfs

4.3.10 – configdist

4.3.11 – confignet

4.3.11.1 – dhcp

4.3.11.2 – manual

4.3.12 – mountdist

4.3.13 – copydist

4.3.14 – sysname

4.3.15 – tzsetup

4.3.16 – bootsetup

4.3.17 – finish

4.4 – Encrypted Partitions

5 – Building the System from Source

5.1 – Why should I build my system from source?

5.2 – Building 9front from source

5.2.1 – Update sources

5.2.1.1 – hgrc

5.2.1.2 – git

5.2.2 – Building from source

5.2.2.1 – Cross compiling

5.3 – Building an ISO

5.4 – Common Problems when Compiling and Building

5.4.1 – Upgrading compilers

6 – Networking

6.1 – Before we go any further

6.2 – Network configuration

6.2.1 – Host name

6.2.2 – Identifying and setting up your network interfaces

6.2.2.1 – WiFi

6.2.2.1.1 – Interfaces

6.2.2.1.1.1 – wavelan

6.2.2.1.1.2 – wavelanpci

6.2.2.1.1.3 – iwl

6.2.2.1.1.4 – rt2860

6.2.2.1.1.5 – wpi

6.2.2.1.2 – WPA

6.2.2.1.3 – WiFi Roaming

6.2.2.1.4 – WiFi Debug

6.2.3 – IP address

6.2.4 – Default gateway

6.2.5 – DNS Resolution

6.2.5.1 – Caching DNS server

6.2.5.2 – DNS authoritative name server

6.2.5.2.1 – Troubleshooting DNS authoritative name server

6.2.6 – Network-wide configuration

6.2.7 – Activating the changes

6.2.7.1 – NIC

6.2.7.2 – cs

6.2.7.3 – dns

6.2.8 – Verifying network settings

6.2.8.1 – Checking routes

6.2.8.1.1 – Adding static routes

6.2.9 – Setting up your 9front box as a forwarding gateway

6.2.10 – Setting up aliases on an interface

6.3 – How do I filter and firewall with 9front?

6.4 – Dynamic Host Configuration Protocol (DHCP)

6.4.1 – DHCP client

6.4.2 – DHCP server

6.5 – PPP

6.6 – Setting up a network bridge in 9front

6.7 – How do I boot from the network?

6.7.1 – How do I tcp boot?

6.7.1.1 – Passing arguments to ipconfig at the bootargs prompt

6.7.2 – How do I boot using PXE?

7 – System Management

7.1 – Plan 9 Services Overview

7.1.1 – What is the kernel?

7.1.2 – What is the file server?

7.1.3 – What is the auth server?

7.1.4 – What is the cpu server?

7.1.5 – What is a terminal?

7.2 – Kernel configuration and maintenance

7.2.1 – How do I mount the 9fat partition?

7.2.2 – How do I modify plan9.ini?

7.2.3 – Kernel configuration file

7.2.4 – Kernel drivers

7.2.5 – How do I install a new kernel?

7.3 – Fileserver configuration and maintenance

7.3.1 – Adding users

7.3.2 – Configuring nvram

7.3.3 – Setting up a listener for network connections

7.3.3.1 – Stop cwfs from allowing user none to attach without authentication

7.3.3.1.1 – notes on user none

7.3.4 – Mounting a file system from userspace

7.3.5 – dump

7.3.5.1 – manually trigger the dump

7.4 – Auth server configuration and maintenance

7.4.1 – Configuring an auth server

7.4.1.1 – Avoiding an ndb entry for the auth server

7.4.2 – Adding users

7.4.3 – secstored

7.4.3.1 – Adding users to secstore

7.4.3.2 – Converting from p9sk1 to dp9ik

7.5 – Cpu server configuration and maintenance

7.5.1 – Configuring a cpu server

7.6 – Terminal configuration and maintenance

7.6.1 – Configuring a terminal

7.6.2 – Configuring a Terminal to Accept cpu Connections

7.6.3 – UTC Timesync

7.7 – Mail server configuration and maintenance

7.7.1 – smtpd.conf

7.7.2 – rewrite

7.7.3 – names.local

7.7.4 – remotemail

7.7.5 – SMTP over TLS

7.7.6 – IMAP4 over TLS

7.7.7 – Spam Filtering

7.7.7.1 – ratfs

7.7.7.2 – scanmail

7.7.8 – Troubleshooting the mail server

7.7.9 – Setting up a mailing list

7.7.9.1 – mlmgr

7.8 – Web server configuration and maintenance

7.8.1 – ip/httpd

7.8.2 – rc–httpd

7.9 – TLS certificates

8 – Using 9front

8.1 – rc

8.1.1 – Prompts

8.1.2 – /env

8.2 – rio

8.2.1 – The Pop–up Menu

8.2.2 – Window control

8.2.3 – Text in rio windows

8.2.4 – Scrolling

8.2.5 – Mouse Chording

8.2.6 – Keyboard Shortcuts

8.2.7 – Color scheme

8.2.8 – Why is rio like this?

8.2.9 – tips

8.2.9.1 – Taking a screenshot

8.2.9.2 – Prevent console messages from overwriting the screen

8.3 – Text Editors

8.3.1 – sam

8.3.1.1 – Scrolling

8.3.1.2 – Mouse Chording

8.3.1.3 – Why does sam have a separate snarf buffer from rio?

8.3.1.4 – Keyboard Shortcuts

8.3.2 – acme

8.4 – Internet

8.4.1 – Mail

8.4.1.1 – upasfs

8.4.1.1.1 – Reading gmail via IMAP

8.4.1.1.2 – Sending mail with gmail

8.4.1.2 – nedmail

8.4.1.2.1 – mother

8.4.1.2.2 – Nail

8.4.1.3 – nupas

8.4.2 – NNTP

8.4.3 – IRC

8.4.3.1 – ircrc

8.4.3.2 – irc7

8.4.3.3 – ircs

8.4.3.4 – wircrc

8.4.4 – FTP

8.4.5 – HTTP

8.4.5.1 – mothra

8.4.5.2 – abaco

8.4.5.3 – hget

8.4.5.4 – charon

8.4.5.5 – i

8.4.5.6 – NetSurf

8.4.6 – SSH

8.4.6.1 – ssh

8.4.6.1.1 – sshfs

8.4.6.1.2 – sshnet

8.4.6.2 – ssh2

8.4.6.3 – scpu

8.4.6.3.1 – Public Key Authentication

8.4.6.4 – OpenSSH

8.4.6.5 – sftpfs

8.4.6.5.1 – Mounting a remote u9fs share over SSH

8.4.7 – secstore

8.4.8 – drawterm

8.4.8.1 – Connect to Plan 9 from a mobile device

8.4.8.2 – drawterm behind firewalls

8.4.9 – Peer to Peer (P2P)

8.4.9.1 – Tinc

8.4.9.2 – Torrents

8.4.9.2.1 – ip/torrent

8.4.9.2.2 – torrent

8.5 – Audio

8.6 – External Media

8.6.1 – Mount an ISO9660 CD-ROM

8.6.2 – Burn a CD-ROM

8.6.3 – Mount a FAT formatted USB device

8.7 – Emulation

8.7.1 – Linux Emulation

8.7.2 – Nintendo

8.7.3 – Sega

8.7.4 – Commodore

8.7.5 – PC

8.7.5.1 – Virtualization Using vmx(1)

8.7.5.1.1 Block Devices

8.7.5.1.2 Ethernet

8.7.5.1.3 OpenBSD

8.7.5.1.4 Linux

8.7.5.1.5 Windows NT

8.8 – Additional Software

8.8.1 – 9front sources server

8.8.2 – 9front contrib

8.8.3 – Other public 9p servers

8.8.4 – Advanced Namespace Tools for Plan 9

8.8.5 – Even More Additional Software

8.8.6 – Community Maintained Link For Additional Software

8.9 – Bootstrapping architectures not included on the ISO

8.9.1 – amd64

8.9.2 – Raspberry Pi

8.9.3 – arm64

8.10 – ACPI

8.10.1 – Enabling ACPI

8.12 – Revision Control

8.12.1 – cvs

8.12.2 – git

8.12.3 – Mercurial

8.12.4 – svn

8.13 – Video

8.13.1 – treason

9 – Troubleshooting

9.1 – First

9.2 – Booting

9.2.2 – Break into a shell

9.2.3 – Editing plan9.ini

9.2.4 – Boot media not recognized

9.2.5 – I moved my hard drive between ports

9.3 – Graphics

9.3.1 – Rio fails to start

9.3.2 – VESA BIOS does not contain a valid mode

9.4 – Networking

9.4.1 – Networking is not working

9.4.2 – Cannot resolve domain names

9.4.3 – /mnt/web/clone does not exist

9.4.4 – PCMCIA WiFi stopped working after reboot

9.5 – USB

9.5.1 – Devices not recognized or not working

9.5.2 – System freezes after showing memory sizes

9.6 – auth

9.99999999999999999999999999999999999999 – GIVE UP

Appendix

B – Bounties

G – GSOC

J – Junk

L – Languages

T – TODO

Z – Getting Started With 9front

FQA 0 – Introduction to Plan 9

0.1 – What is Plan 9?

Plan 9 is a research operating system from the same group who created UNIX at Bell Labs Computing Sciences Research Center (CSRC). It emerged in the late 1980s, and its early development coincided with continuing development of the later versions of Research UNIX. Plan 9 can be seen as an attempt to push some of the same ideas that informed UNIX *even further* into the era of networking and graphics. Rob Pike has described Plan 9 as "an argument" for simplicity and clarity, while others have described it as "UNIX, only moreso."

From *The Use of Name Spaces in Plan 9:*

Plan 9 argues that given a few carefully implemented abstractions it is possible to produce a small operating system that provides support for the largest systems on a variety of architectures and networks.

From the `intro(1)` man page:

Plan 9 is a distributed computing environment assembled from separate machines acting as terminals, CPU servers, and file servers. A user works at a terminal, running a window system on a raster display. Some windows are connected to CPU servers; the intent is that heavy computing should be done in those windows but it is also possible to compute on the terminal. A separate file server provides file storage for terminals and CPU servers alike.

The two most important ideas in Plan 9 are:

• private namespaces (each process constructs a unique view of the hierarchical file system)

• file interfaces (familiar from UNIX, but taken to the extreme: all resources in Plan 9 look like file systems)

Most everything else in the system falls out of these two basic ideas.

Plan 9 really pushes hard on some ideas that Unix has that haven't really been fully developed, in particular, the notion that just about everything in the system is accessible through a file. In other words, things look like an ordinary disk file. So all the devices are controlled this way by means of ASCII strings, not complicated data structures. For example, you make network calls by writing an ASCII string, not the files. This notion is something that's actually leaking quite fast.

The second thing is sort of more subtle and sort of hard to appreciate until you've actually played with it. That is that the set of files an individual program can see depends on that program itself. In a standard kind of system, either with Unix remote file systems or Windows attached file systems, all the programs running in the machine see the same thing. In Plan 9, that's adjustable per program. You can set up specialized name stations that are unique to a particular program. I mean, it's not associated with the program itself but with the process, with the execution of the process.

— Dennis Ritchie

Read: `intro(1)`; *Plan 9 from Bell Labs; Designing Plan 9*, originally delivered at the UKUUG Conference in London, July 1990; and *FQA 7 – System Management;* for a more detailed overview of Plan 9's design.

Today, Plan 9 continues in its original form, as well as in several derivatives and forks.

The United States of Plan 9

Plan 9 from Bell Labs — The original Plan 9. Effectively dead, all the developers have been run out of the Labs and/or are on display at Google.

Plan 9 from User Space — Plan 9 userspace ported/imitated for UNIX (specifically OS X).

9legacy — David du Colombier's cherry picked collection of patches from various people/forks to Bell Labs Plan 9. (it is not a fork)

9atom — Erik Quanstrom's fork of Plan 9, maintained to erik's needs and occasionally pilfered by 9front.

9front — (that's us) (we rule (we're the tunnel snakes))

NIX — High performance cloud computing is NIX — imploded in a cloud of political acrimony and retarded bureaucratic infighting.

NxM — A kernel for manycore systems — never spotted in the wild.

Clive — A new operating system from Francisco J. Ballesteros, designed to generate grantwriting practice material and research projects for otherwise indolent students.

Akaros — Akaros is an open source, GPL-licensed operating system for manycore architectures. Has no bearing on anything but has attracted grant money.

Harvey — Harvey is an effort to get the Plan 9 code working with gcc and clang.

Inferno — Inferno is a distributed operating system started at Bell Labs, but is now developed and maintained by Vita Nuova Holdings as free software. Just kidding it is not developed or maintained.

ANTS — Advanced Namespace Tools for Plan 9. ANTS is a collection of modifications and additional software which adds new namespace manipulation capabilities to Plan 9.

Jehanne — Jehanne:Harvey::William King Harvey:J. Edgar Hoover

Plan 9 Foundation — Now offering downloads of historical Plan 9 releases.

0.1.1 – Plan 9 is not UNIX

In the words of the Bell Labs Plan 9 wiki:

> Plan 9 is not Unix. If you think of it as Unix, you may become frustrated when something doesn't exist or when it works differently than you expected. If you think of it as Plan 9, however, you'll find that most of it works very smoothly, and that there are some truly neat ideas that make things much cleaner than you have seen before.

Confusion is compounded by the fact that many UNIX commands exist on Plan 9 and behave in similar ways. In fact, some of Plan 9's userland (such as the upas mail interface, the sam text editor, and the rc shell) are carried over directly from Research UNIX 10th Edition. Further investigation reveals that many ideas found in Plan 9 were explored in more primitive form in the later editions of Research UNIX.

However, Plan 9 is a completely new operating system that makes no attempt to conform to past prejudices. The point of the exercise (circa the late 1980s) was to avoid past problems and explore new territory. Plan 9 is not UNIX *for a reason.*

Read: *UNIX to Plan 9 command translation, UNIX Style, or cat –v Considered Harmful*

0.1.1.1 – Plan 9 is not plan9port

Plan 9 from User Space (also known as plan9port or p9p) is a port of many Plan 9 from Bell Labs libraries and applications to UNIX–like operating systems. Currently it has been tested on a variety of operating systems including: Linux, Mac OS X, FreeBSD, NetBSD, OpenBSD, Solaris and SunOS.

Plan9port consists of a combination of mostly unaltered Plan 9 userland utilities packaged alongside various attempts to imitate Plan 9's kernel intefaces using miscellaneous available UNIX programs and commands. Some of the imitations are more successful than others. In all, plan9port does not accurately represent the experience of using actual Plan 9, but does provide enough functionality to make some users content with running acme on their Macbooks.

It is now being slowly ported to the Go programming language.

0.1.1.2 – Plan 9 is not Inferno

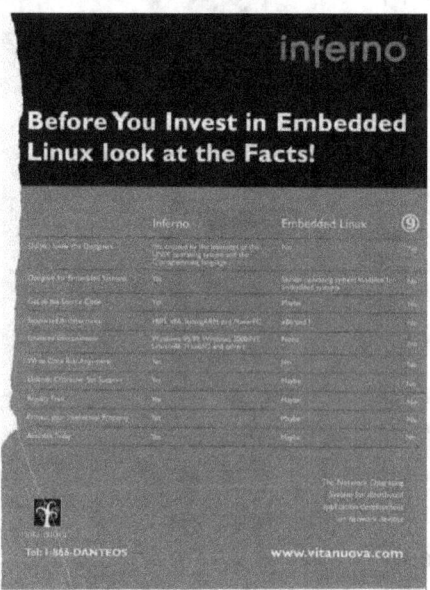

Inferno is a distributed operating system also created at Bell Labs, but which is now developed and maintained by Vita Nuova Holdings as free software. It employs many ideas from Plan 9 (and even shares some source code), but is a completely different OS.

Note: Inferno shares some compatible interfaces with Plan 9, including the 9P/Styx protocol.

0.1.2 – Plan 9 is not a product

Path: utzoo!utgpu!water!watmath!clyde!bellcore!faline!thumper!ulysses!smb
From: s...@ulysses.homer.nj.att.com (Steven Bellovin)
Newsgroups: comp.unix.wizards
Subject: Re: Plan 9? (+ others)
Message-ID: <10533@ulysses.homer.nj.att.com>
Date: 23 Aug 88 16:19:40 GMT
References: <846@yunexus.UUCP> <282@umbio.MIAMI.EDU> <848@yunexus.UUCP>
Organization: AT&T Bell Laboratories, Murray Hill
Lines: 33

"Plan 9" is not a product, and is not intended to be. It is research --
an experimental investigation into a different way of computing. The
developers started from several basic assumptions: that CPUs are very
cheap but that we don't really know how to combine them effectively; that
good networking is very important; that an intelligent user interface
(complete with dot-mapped display and mouse) is a Right Decision; that
existing systems with networks, mice, etc., are not the correct way to
do things, and in particular that today's workstations are not the way to
go. (No, I won't bother to explain all their reasoning; that's a long
and separate article.) Finally, the UNIX system per se is dead as a
vehicle for serious research into operating system structure; it has grown
too large, and is too constrained by 15+ years of history.

Now -- given those assumptions, they decided to throw away what we have
today and design a new system. Compatibility isn't an issue -- they are
not in the product-building business. (Nor are they in the "let's make
another clever hack" business.) Of course aspects of Plan 9 resemble
the UNIX system quite strongly -- is it any surprise that Pike, Thompson,
et al., think that that's a decent model to follow? But Plan 9 isn't,
and is not meant to be, a re-implementation of the UNIX system. If you
want, call it a UNIX-like system.

Will Plan 9 ever be released? I have no idea. Will it remain buried?
I hope not. Large companies do not sponsor large research organizations
just for the prestige; they hope for an (eventual) concrete return in the
form of concepts that can be made into (or incorporated into) products.

      --Steve Bellovin

Disclaimer: this article is not, of course, an official statement from AT&T.
Nor is it an official statement of the reasoning behind Plan 9. I do think
it's accurate, though, and I'm sure I'll be told if I'm wrong...

0.1.3 – Plan 9 is not for you

Let's be perfectly honest. Many features that today's "computer experts" consider to
be essential to computing (javascript, CSS, HTML5, etc.) either did not exist when Plan 9
was abandoned, or were purposely left out of the operating system. You might find this
to be an unacceptable obstacle to adopting Plan 9 into your daily workflow. If you

cannot imagine a use for a computer that does not involve a web browser, Plan 9 may not be for you.

See: http://harmful.cat-v.org/software/

On the other hand, the roaring 2020s have seen Plan 9 sprout a substantial presence on social media, so if you're here for that, YMMV.

0.2 – Why Plan 9?

You may ask yourself, well, how did I get here? In the words of Plan 9 contributor Russ Cox:

> Why Plan 9 indeed. Isn't Plan 9 just another Unix clone? Who cares?
>
> Plan 9 presents a consistent and easy to use interface. Once you've settled in, there are very few surprises here. After I switched to Linux from Windows 3.1, I noticed all manner of inconsistent behavior in Windows 3.1 that Linux did not have. Switching to Plan 9 from Linux highlighted just as much in Linux.
>
> One reason Plan 9 can do this is that the Plan 9 group has had the luxury of having an entire system, so problems can be fixed and features added where they belong, rather than where they can be. For example, there is no tty driver in the kernel. The window system handles the nuances of terminal input.
>
> If Plan 9 was just a really clean Unix clone, it might be worth using, or it might not. The neat things start happening with user-level file servers and per-process namespace. In Unix, /dev/tty refers to the current window's output device, and means different things to different processes. This is a special hack enabled by the kernel for a single file. Plan 9 provides full-blown per-

process namespaces. In Plan 9 /dev/cons also refers to the current window's output device, and means different things to different processes, but the window system (or telnet daemon, or ssh daemon, or whatever) arranges this, and does the same for /dev/mouse, /dev/text (the contents of the current window), etc.

Since pieces of file tree can be provided by user-level servers, the kernel need not know about things like DOS's FAT file system or GNU/Linux's EXT2 file system or NFS, etc. Instead, user-level servers provide this functionality when desired. In Plan 9, even FTP is provided as a file server: you run ftpfs and the files on the server appear in /n/ftp.

We need not stop at physical file systems, though. Other file servers synthesize files that represent other resources. For example, upas/fs presents your mail box as a file tree at /mail/fs/mbox. This models the recursive structure of MIME messages especially well.

As another example, cdfs presents an audio or data CD as a file system, one file per track. If it's a writable CD, copying new files into the /mnt/cd/wa or /mnt/cd/wd directories does create new audio or data tracks. Want to fixate the CD as audio or data? Remove one of the directories.

Plan 9 fits well with a networked environment, files and directory trees can be imported from other machines, and all resources are files or directory trees, it's easy to share resources. Want to use a different machine's sound card? Import its /dev/audio. Want to debug processes that run on another machine? Import its /proc. Want to use a network interface on another machine? Import its /net. And so on.

Russ Cox

0.2.1 – What do people like about Plan 9?

Descriptive testmony by long time Plan 9 users Charles Forstyh, Anthony Sorace and Geoff Collyer:

https://9p.io/wiki/plan9/what_do_people_like_about_plan_9/index.html

0.2.1.1 – What do you use Plan 9 for?

Computing.

Read: *How I Switched To Plan 9*

See: *FQA 8 – Using 9front*

0.2.2 – What do people hate about Plan 9?

John floren provides a humorous(?) overview of a typical new user's reactions to Plan 9:

Hi! I'm new to Plan 9. I'm really excited to work with this new Linux system.

I hit some questions.
1 How do I run X11?
2 Where is Emacs?
3 The code is weird. It doesn't look like GNU C at all. Did the people who wrote Plan 9 know about C?
4 I tried to run mozilla but it did not work. How come?

Is this guy you?

Related: http://9front.org/buds.html

0.2.2.1 – What is not in Plan 9

A summary of common features you may have been expecting that are missing from Plan 9:

http://c2.com/cgi/wiki?WhatIsNotInPlanNine

0.2.3 – Why did Plan 9's creators give up on Plan 9?

All of the people who worked on Plan 9 have moved on from Bell Labs and/or no longer work on Plan 9. Various reasons have been articulated by various people.

Russ Cox:

I ran Plan 9 from Bell Labs as my day to day work environment until around 2002. By then two facts were painfully clear. First, the Internet was here to stay; and second, Plan 9 had no hope of keeping up with web browsers. Porting Mozilla to Plan 9 was far too much work, so instead I ported almost all the Plan 9 user level software to FreeBSD, Linux, and OS X.

Russ Cox (again):

The standard set up for a Plan 9 aficionado here seems to be a Mac or Linux machine running Plan 9 from User Space to get at sam, acme, and the other tools. Rob, Ken, Dave, and I use Macs as our desktop machines, but we're a bit of an exception. Most Google engineers use Linux machines, and I know of quite a few ex-Bell Labs people who are happy to be using sam or acme on those machines. My own setup is two screens. The first is a standard Mac desktop with non-Plan 9 apps and a handful of 9terms, and the second is a full-screen acme for getting work done. On Linux I do the same but the first screen is a Linux desktop running rio (formerly dhog's 8½).

More broadly, every few months I tend to get an email from someone who is happy to have just discovered that sam is still maintained and available for modern systems. A lot of the time these are people who only used sam on Unix, never on Plan 9. The plan9port.tgz file was downloaded from 2,522 unique IP addresses in 2009, which I suspect is many more than Plan 9 itself. In that sense, it's really nice to see the tools getting a much wider exposure than they used to.

I haven't logged into a real Plan 9 system in many years, but I use 9vx occasionally when I want to remind myself how a real Plan 9 tool worked. It's always nice to be back, however briefly.

Russ

Russ Cox continues:

> Can you briefly tell us why you (Russ, Rob, Ken and Dave)
> no longer use Plan9 ?
> Because of missing apps or because of missing driver for your hardware ?
> And do you still use venti ?

Operating systems and programming languages have strong network effects: it helps to use the same system that everyone around you is using. In my group at MIT, that meant FreeBSD and C++. I ran Plan 9 for the first few years I was at MIT but gave up, because the lack of a shared system made it too hard to collaborate. When I switched to FreeBSD, I ported all the Plan 9 libraries and tools so I could keep the rest of the user experience.

I still use venti, in that I still maintain the venti server that takes care of backups for my old group at MIT. It uses the plan9port venti, vbackup, and vnfs, all running on FreeBSD. The venti server itself was my last real Plan 9 installation. It's Coraid hardware, but I stripped the software and had installed my own Plan 9 kernel to run venti on it directly. But before I left MIT, the last thing I did was reinstall the machine using FreeBSD so that others could help keep it up to date.

If I wasn't interacting with anyone else it'd be nice to keep using Plan 9. But it's also nice to be able to use off the shelf software instead of reinventing wheels (9fans runs on Linux) and to have good hardware support done by other people (I can shut my laptop and it goes to sleep, and even better, when I open it again, it wakes up!). Being able to get those things and still keep most of the Plan 9 user experience by running Plan 9 from User Space is a compromise, but one that works well for me.

Russ

Rob Pike:

What Russ says is true but for me it was simpler. I used Plan 9 as my local operating system for a year or so after joining Google, but it was just too inconvenient to live on a machine without a C++ compiler, without good NFS and SSH support, and especially without a web browser. I switched to Linux but found it very buggy (the main problem was most likely a bad graphics board and/or driver, but still) and my main collaborator (Robert Griesemer) had done the ground work to get a Mac working as a primary machine inside Google, and Russ had plan9port up, so I pushed plan9port onto the Mac and have been there ever since, quite happily. Nowadays Apples are officially supported so it's become easy, workwise.

I miss a lot of what Plan 9 did for me, but the concerns at work override that.

-rob

0.2.3.1 – Why did Plan 9's users give up on Plan 9?

They probably have their reasons.

0.2.3.2 – Why did CIA give up on Plan 9?

Someone tried to find out:

https://www.muckrock.com/foi/united-states-of-america-10/foia-cia-plan-9-from-bell-labs-82547/

0.2.4 – What is the deal with Plan 9's weird license?

Over the years Plan 9 has been released under various licenses, to the consternation of many.

The first edition, released in 1992, was made available only to universities. The process for acquiring the software was convoluted and prone to clerical error. Many potential users had trouble obtaining it within a reasonable time frame and many complaints were voiced on the eventual Plan 9 Internet mailing list.

The second edition, released in 1995 in book-and-CD form under a relatively standard commercial license, was available via mailorder as well as through a special telephone number for a price of approximately $350 USD. It was certainly easier to acquire than the first edition, but many potential users still complained that the price was too high and that the license was too restrictive.

0.2.4.1 – Richard Stallman hates the Plan Nine license (circa 2000)

In the year 2000, the third edition of Plan 9 was finally released under a custom "open source" license, the Plan 9 License. Richard Stallman was not impressed:

> When I saw the announcement that the Plan Nine software had been released as "open source", I wondered whether it might be free software as well. After studying the license, my conclusion was that it is not free; the license contains several restrictions that are totally unacceptable for the Free Software Movement. (See http://www.gnu.org/philosophy/free-sw.html

Read more here:

http://www.linuxtoday.com/developer/2000070200704OPLFSW

0.2.4.2 – Theo de Raadt hates the Plan 9 license (circa 2003)

In the year 2002, the fourth edition of Plan 9 was released under the Lucent Public License. This time, Theo de Raadt was not impressed:

> The new license is utterly unacceptable for use in a BSD project.
>
> Actually, I am astounded that the OSI would declare such a license acceptable.
>
> That is not a license which makes it free. It is a *contract* with consequences; let me be clear -- it is a contract with consequences that I am unwilling to accept.

Read more here:

http://9fans.net/archive/2003/06/270

0.2.4.3 – Everyone hates the Plan 9 license (circa 2014)

In 2014, portions of the Plan 9 source code were again re-licensed, this time under the GPLv2, for distribution with the University of California, Berkeley's Akaros operating system. Predictably, various parties were not impressed.

Russ Cox tried to make sense of the situation by commenting in a Hacker News thread:

> When you ask "why did big company X make strange choice Y regarding licensing or IP", 99 times out of 100 the answer is "lawyers". If the Plan 9 group had had its way, Plan 9 would have been released for free under a trivial MIT-like license (the one used for other pieces of code, like the one true awk) in 2003 instead of creating the Lucent Public License. Or in 2000 instead of creating the "Plan 9 License". Or in 1995 instead of as a $350 book+CD that came with a license for use by an entire "organization". Or in 1992 instead of being a limited academic release.
>
> Thankfully I am not at Lucent anymore and am not privy to the tortured negotiations that ended up at the obviously inelegant compromise of "The University of California, Berkeley, has been authorised by Alcatel-Lucent to release all Plan 9 software previously governed by the Lucent Public License, Version 1.02 under the GNU General Public License, Version 2." But the odds are overwhelming that the one-word answer is "lawyers".

Some have suggested that confusion about licensing may have contributed to Plan 9's failure to supplant UNIX in the wider computing world.

0.2.4.4 – PRAISE FOR 9FRONT'S BOLD ACTION RE: LICENSING

Any additions or changes (as recorded in Mercurial history) made by 9front are provided under the terms of the MIT License, reproduced in the file /lib/legal/mit, unless otherwise indicated.

Read: /lib/legal/NOTICE.

0.2.4.5 – Everyone loves the Plan 9 license (circa 2021)

In 2021, the Plan 9 Foundation (aka P9F—no relation) convinced Nokia to re-license all historical editions of the Plan9 source code under the MIT Public License.

As a consequence, *all* of 9front is now provided under the MIT License unless otherwise indicated.

Re-read: `/lib/legal/mit`

0.3 – Further Reading

0.3.1 – Plan 9 papers

Academic papers that describe the Plan 9 operating system are available here:

http://doc.cat-v.org/plan_9/

0.3.2 – Man pages

Section (1) for general publicly accessible commands.

Section (2) for library functions, including system calls.

Section (3) for kernel devices (accessed via bind(1)).

Section (4) for file services (accessed via mount).

Section (5) for the Plan 9 file protocol.

Section (6) for file formats.

Section (7) for databases and database access programs.

Section (8) for things related to administering Plan 9.

0.3.3 – Web pages

The official website for the Plan 9 project is located at: https://9p.io/wiki/plan9

The official website for the Plan 9 Foundation is located at: http://p9f.org

The 9front fork of Plan 9 (that's us): http://9front.org

A community wiki setup by 9front users: http://wiki.a-b.xyz

Much other valuable information can be found at http://cat-v.org regarding aspects of UNIX, Plan 9, and software in general.

Introduction to OS Abstractions Using Plan 9 From Bell Labs, by Francisco J Ballestros (nemo)

Notes on the Plan 9 3rd Edition Kernel, by Francisco J Ballestros (nemo)

The UNIX Programming Environment, by Brian W. Kernighan (bwk) and Rob Pike (rob) (this book is the most clear, concise and eloquent expression of the Unix and 'tool' philosophies to date)

9FRONT DASH 1 (the document you are reading right now, but in book form)

9front System

1.1 – What is 9front?

Plan9front (or 9front) is a fork of the Plan 9 from Bell Labs operating system. The project was started to remedy a perceived lack of devoted development resources inside Bell Labs,[citation needed] and has accumulated various fixes and improvements.

This FQA specifically covers only the most recent release of 9front.

1.1.1 – Cirno

At some point, Cirno became associated with 9front. Details are sketchy, but this image has been in the wiki since the Google Code days, so I'm leaving it in.

Pro

- girl

- has magical powers

- associated with 9

- upsets kfx

- she is known to be the strongest

Alternatives

1.2 – On what systems does 9front run?

9front runs on the following platforms:

- 386

- amd64

- arm

- arm64

• mips

Read: *FQA 3.2 – Selecting Hardware*

1.3 – Why might I want to use 9front?

It is very likely that you do not.

New users frequently want to know whether 9front is superior to some other free UNIX-like operating system. Consider: The question is largely unanswerable. What are your criteria? Why are you even using computers in the first place? Exploring these questions and the implications that derive therefrom may help you sharpen your perceptions and eventually come to some sort of conclusion about which operating system you prefer to use for daily tasks.

Ultimately, whether or not 9front is for you is a question only you can answer.

Note: The above text is lightly plagiarized from the OpenBSD FAQ.

1.3.0 – Why might I not want to use 9front?

Hold up. Before you get too excited, consider the following possibilities:

• You just realized you don't want to use Plan 9 at all.

• You don't like the people who use and/or work on 9front.

• You don't like 9front's propaganda.

• You prefer less functionality from your obscure OS, and/or you prefer to ignore 9front's public commit history and complain later because nobody informed you about bug fixes and new programs.

• You have technical objections to specific changes 9front made to the original Bell Labs code.

• You're not sure right now, but you'll know it when you see it.

Okay, carry on.

1.3.0.1 – Why did 9front stop making fun of Nazis?

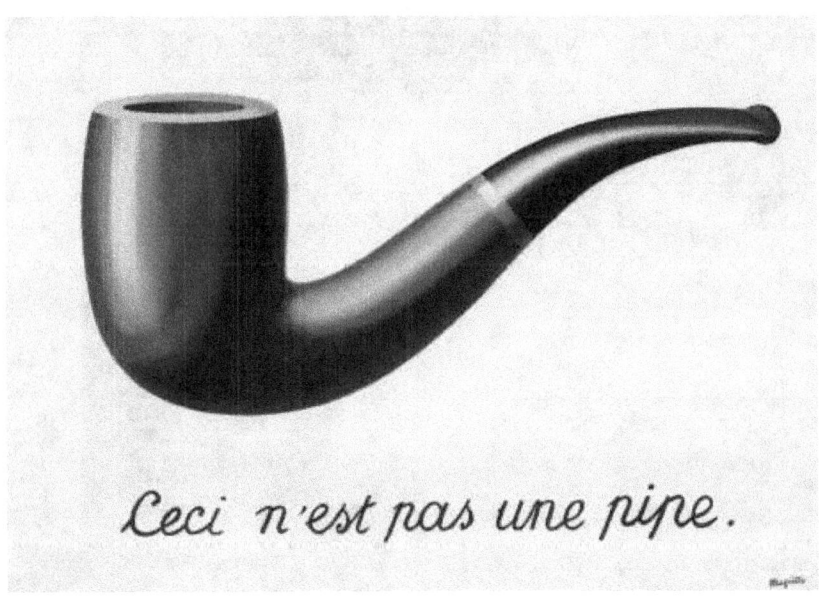

Because you asked us to.

- People complained it was done in poor taste.

- People reliably interpret any depiction of a thing as an endorsement of same.

- We're tired of explaining this shit to people who just call us liars anyway. (To be fair, look at the world around us today. Why cloud the issue?) *I'm through explainin the shit —Ice T*

- Cognitive dissonance.

Read: *Appendix L – Ruby*

Possibly related: *Der Anbräuner*

Definitely relevant: *They Live and the secret history of the Mozilla logo*

This poor guy: *Anselm Kiefer*

1.3.1 – New Features

The following list is probably not exhaustive:

- /shr, global mountpoint device shr(3)

- /mnt is provided by mntgen(4)

- #A, audio drivers for sb16, intel hd audio and ac97 (both playback and recording supported!) audio(3)

- New BIOS based boot loader 9boot(8) featuring a console and support for FAT/ISO/PXE and being small (<8K)

- New EFI based boot loader efi

- Made kernel compliant to multiboot specification so it can be booted by qemu or grub directly.

- Interruptable kernel qlocks (eqlock)

- Defered clunks (closeproc) for cached mounts

- New rc based boot(8) allows breaking into a shell at any time

- Default file system is an improved cwfs(4) (cwfs64x)

- New screen fonts: dejavu, germgoth, vga

- No central replica; source updates are done with git(1) (Mercurial)

- Keyboard events with /dev/kbd. Read: kbdfs(8) and rio(4)

- `/lib/rob` and other new corpuses, suitable as fodder for `fortune(1)` and other rhetorical programs

- New `listen(8) -p maxprocs` option

- Always available network `aan(8)` support in `cpu(1)` and `rcpu(1)`

- MSI (message signalled interrupts), avoids problems with broken MP tables. Read: `icanhasmsi(8)`

- Legacy free ACPI support (aml interpreter `libaml`, mp interrupt routing, `scram`)

- Added `rio(1) -b` option (black window backgrounds) and `look` menu option

- USB CD-ROM boot/install

- USB drive boot

- Improved USB mouse support

- Support for USB ptp cameras

- Stable-across-machines USB device names

- VGA initialization done by interpreting the VESA BIOS with `realemu(8)`, working VESA screen blanking.

- `/dev/kbd` and clipboard charset support for `vnc(1)`

- New `webfs(4)` with HTTP1.1 and Keep-Alive support.

- Qemu/KVM virtio block device and ethernet drivers. Read: *FQA 4.5.1.3 — Virtio*

- Mouse wheel and chording support in `sam(1)`

- Elliptic curve cryptography `ec(2)`

- Working interrupt key (Del) in console

- WiFi support with wpa/wpa2

- SSE support

- System-wide support for internationalized domain names

- Unicode support in `vt(1)`

- `pc64`, kernel for amd64

- Numerous ciphers added and improvements made to `libsec`

- New dpi9k authentication protocol

43

1.3.1.1 – New Programs

- `"` and `""` (print, repeat previous command)

- `alarm(1)` — timeouts in `rc` scripts

- `atari(1)` — 2600 emulator

- `audio(1)` — `mp3`, `ogg`, `flac`, `μlaw`, `wav`

- `blit(1)` — Blit terminal emulator

- `bullshit(1)` — print out a stream of bullshit

- `cifsd(8)` — CIFS/SMB server

- `cryptsetup(8)` — prepare an AES-encrypted partition to be used with the `fs(3)` device

- `derp(1)` — find changes between directories

- `dtracy(1)` — dynamic tracing language (like dtrace)

- `feminize(1)` — replace sexist remarks

- `fplot(1)`

- New games: `doom`, `glendy`, `linden`, `mandel`, `mines`, `mole`, `packet`, `v8e`

- `git(1)` — native git client

- `hget(1)` — rewritten in `rc`, now uses `webfs`

- `hjfs(4)` — new, experimental fs

- `hpost(1)` — extract and post HTML forms

- `hold(1)` — simple text editor

- `icanhasmsi(8)` — print MSI configuration

- `ipserv(8)` — proxy servers `socksd` and `hproxy`

- `ircrc(1)` — IRC client

- `memory(1)` — check memory usage

- `mothra(1)` — Tom Duff's web browser, now uses `webfs`

- `netaudit(8)` — network configuration checker

- `newt(1)` — Usenet client

- `nietzsche(1)` — print out Nietzsche quote

- `nintendo(1)` — Nintendo emulators: gb, gba, nes, snes

- `page(1)` — zoom and enhance!

- `paint(1)` — drawing program

- `play(1)` — audio player

- `pstree(1)` — print tree-like map of current processes and sub-processes

- `ptrap(4)` — plumber(4) filter

- `rc-httpd(8)` — HTTP server

- `rcpu(1)` — replacement for legacy cpu(1) client, uses dp9ik

- `resize(1)` — fast but low quality image resampler

- `rotate(1)` — rotate or mirror a picture

- `scram(8)` — ACPI and APM shutdown

- `sega(1)` — Sega Megadrive/Genesis emulator: md

- `spred(1)` — sprite editor

- `ssam(1)` — stream interface to sam

- `ssh(1)` — SSH2 client

- `sshnet(4)` — re-implementation of sshnet for SSH2

- `sysinfo(1)` — print hardware report

- `sysupdate(1)` — update the local git repository

- `theo(1)` — print out insults from Theo de Raadt

- `tput(1)` — measure read throughput

- `troll(1)` — automated trolling

- `tap(1)` — follow the pipes of a process

- `tif(1)` — tiff decoder

- `tinc(8)` — mesh peer to peer VPN

- `tojpg(1)` — jpeg encoder

- `totif(1)` — tiff encoder

- `torrent(1)` — bittorrent client

- `walk(1)` — recursively walk descending directories

- `zuke(1)` — gui audio player, replacement for juke(1)

1.3.1.1.1 – Why do some new program names begin with hj?

Date: Wed, 8 Mar 2006 15:10:14 +1100
From: "Bruce Ellis" <bruce.ellis@gmail.com>
To: "Fans of the OS Plan 9 from Bell Labs" <9fans@cse.psu.edu>
Subject: Re: [9fans] structure allocation.

i still like hjdicks it is obscure enough that no-one would think it's
a feature (or guess it). it was required because we had a large
slab of 3rd-party code that assumed it could read packets off the
wire (assuming correct endian) and do no marshaling.

#pragam pack

looks like a feature.

i was there when it happened (after a nice italian meal).

ken asked "Do i really have to do this?"

P: Yes, there's buckets of code that rely on it.

K: *some expression of disbelief*

P: well hj are just dicks

done deal

it also turned out to be important for inferno on machines with
greater than 32 bit alignment requirements. the 64 bit mips
is an example. took but a recompile with hjdicks in the right
place (it takes an optional alignment parameter). same with
the ps2 which has 128 bit issues.

thanks for telling me that it has been changed.

brucee

On 3/8/06, geoff@collyer.net <geoff@collyer.net> wrote:
> I was implicitly referring to C compilers. Heck, Pascal had packed
> data in the early 1970s, possibly even the late 1960s.

1.3.1.2 – New Hardware Support

Audio

- AC97 — `/sys/src/9/pc/audioac97.c`
- Intel HDA — `/sys/src/9/pc/audiohda.c`
- SB 16/ESS — `/sys/src/9/pc/audiosb16.c`
- Countless new variants (VID/DID) added to existing drivers.

Ethernet

- ADMtek Pegasus — `/sys/src/cmd/nusb/ether/aue.c`
- Broadcom BCM57xx — `/sys/src/9/pc/etherbcm.c`
- Realtek RTL8150 — `/sys/src/cmd/nusb/ether/url.c`
- Countless new variants (VID/DID) added to existing drivers.

WiFi

- Intel Centrino Advanced-N 6205 (iwl-6005)
- Intel Centrino Ultimate-N (iwl-6000)
- Intel Centrino Wireless-N 100
- Intel WiFi Link 1000/4965/5100/5300/5350 AGN
- Intel PRO Wireless 3945ABG (wpi-3945abg)
- Intel Wireless AC 8260/8265
- Intel Wireless AC 9260
- Ralink RT2860/RT3090

Tablets

- Wacom serial tablets WACF004, WACF008

`/sys/src/cmd/aux/wacom.c`, `/sys/src/cmd/aux/tablet.c`

- USB tablets supported by USB subsystem

Video

- AMD Geode LX driver

  `/sys/src/cmd/aux/vga/geode.c /sys/src/9/pc/vgageode.c`

- Intel GM915, GM965, Sandy Bridge, Ivy Bridge, and Haswell driver

  `/sys/src/cmd/aux/vga/igfx.c /sys/src/9/pc/vgaigfx.c`

SD Card

- Ricoh — `/sys/src/9/pc/pmmc.c`

Read: *FQA 3.2 – Known Working Hardware* for a list of complete machines known to work.

1.4 – Is 9front really free?

Yes.

Read: *FQA 0.2.4 – What is the deal with Plan 9's weird license?*

1.5 – How can I help support 9front?

We are greatly indebted to the people and organizations that have contributed to the 9front project. That said, the topic is complicated: The main developers refuse to accept donations (except when they do accept donations), and the people who do offer to make donations often disappear without further explanation or make strange demands that

48

nobody feels like capitulating to. This complex, fluid, and at times contentious dynamic can best be navigated by joining `#cat-v` on irc.oftc.net and asking strangers how to donate to the project.

When this fails, donations that help pay for the hosting of `9front.org` and `cat-v.org` (including `fqa.9front.org`, the document you are reading right now) can be made at: `http://patreon.com/stanleylieber`

You can also buy a print copy of the 9front dash1 manual (the print edition of the document you are reading right now), and/or the man pages at: `http://9front.org/propaganda/books`

1.6 – Who maintains 9front?

9front is maintained by an East German intelligence officer who never sleeps, but instead logs periods of inactivity staring straight into the soulless eyes of `games/catclock`. Occasional contributions are made by a diverse team of malcontents that is spread somewhat thinly across many different timezones and Internet providers. Most of them have dayjobs, and in fact are not concerned with your demands. (Subsidized or not).

1.7 – When is the next release of 9front?

Soon.

The 9front team makes new releases on a regular, but unscheduled, basis. More information on the development cycle can be found on the 9front mailing list, while historical release announcements are archived at 9front.org/releases.

1.8 – What is included with 9front?

Some useful programs included with the operating system are:
- 2600 — Atari 2600 emulator.

- `acid` — Programmable symbolic debugger.

- `acme` — Text editor, window system, mail client and more.

- `ape` — ANSI/POSIX environment.

- `cwfs64x` — Cached-worm file server based on the original Ken's fs.

- `doom` — Science fiction horror-themed first-person shooter video game by id Software.

- `git` — native git client.

- `gs` — Aladdin Ghostscript (PostScript and PDF language interpreter).

- `hjfs` — A new, experimental fs.

- mk — Tool for describing and maintaining dependencies between files.

- mothra — Web browser by Tom Duff.

- newt — NNTP client.

- nintendo — Nintendo Game Boy, NES, SNES and GBA emulators.

- paint — Drawing program.

- page — FAX, image, graphic, PostScript, PDF, epub, cbz viewer.

- play — Flac, ogg, mp3, sun, wav player.

- plumber — Mechanism for inter-process communication.

- python 2.5.1 — Interpreted programming language. (needed for mercurial)

- rc — Shell by Tom Duff.

- rc-httpd — Web server written in rc.

- rio — Rectangle multiplexer/window system.

- sam — Text editor.

- sega — Megadrive/Genesis emulator.

- torrent — BitTorrent client.

- troff — Text processor/typesetter.

- upas — A simpler approach to network mail.

- zuke — GUI audio player.

1.9 – Can I use 9front as a desktop system?

This question is often asked in exactly this manner—with no explanation of what the asker means by "desktop". The only person who can answer that question is you, as it depends on what your needs and expectations are.

Read: *FQA 1.3 – Why might I want to use 9front?*

1.10 – Why is/isn't ProductX included?

Two potential reasons:
- Nobody wanted it.

- Nobody wrote the code.

Many "features" and programs are missing from Plan 9 for a very good reason: They are terrible ideas expressed as terrible software. Other features are missing simply because no one has yet written the code to implement them. It is left as an exercise for the reader to determine which is which, and to apply the appropriate remedy.

Read: *FQA 8.8 – Additional Software*

1.11 – Fine, where can I get 9front?

If you simply cannot be dissuaded from trying 9front for yourself, obtain installation media from the mirrors mentioned in the following section.

1.11.1 – Mirrors

1.11.1.1 – 9front.iso

http://9front.org/iso/

http://r-36.net/9front/

http://falloff.net/usr/cinap_lenrek/9front.torrent

https://ftp.cc.uoc.gr/mirrors/9front/

http://fulton.software/9front/

1.11.1.2 – git repository

https://code.9front.org/hg/plan9front (official)

Good luck, you may need it.

FQA 2 – Getting To Know 9front

2.1 – Web Pages

The official websites for the 9front project are located at:

• http://9front.org — main website

• http://wiki.9front.org — unofficial mirror of unofficial documentation, community maintained

• http://fqa.9front.org — counterintelligence manual, ostensibly fictional

• http://lists.9front.org — mailing lists

• http://man.9front.org — man pages

Somewhat outdated, and not entirely applicable to 9front is the Bell Labs Plan 9 wiki: https://9p.io/wiki/plan9/plan_9_wiki/

Some users have set up their own sites and pages with 9front specific information. As always, do not blindly enter commands you do not understand into your computer.

That said, much valuable information can be found at http://cat-v.org regarding various aspects of UNIX, Plan 9, and software in general.

2.2 – Mailing Lists

The 9front project maintains several mailing lists which users should subscribe to and follow. To subscribe to a mailing list, send an e-mail message to *list*-owner@9front.org, where *list* is the name of the mailing list. That address is an automated subscription service. In the body of your message, on a single line, you should include the subscribe command. For example:

```
subscribe
```

After subscribing, list messages are received from and sent to *list*@9front.org, where *list* is the name of the mailing list.

The *lists* are as follows:

9front — general discussion

9front-commits — read-only log of commits to the 9front mercurial repository

9front-fqa — log of commits to, and discussion about `http://fqa.9front.org`

9front-sysinfo — read-only log of `sysinfo(1)` output from user systems

To unsubscribe from a list, you will again send an e-mail message to *list-owner*@9front.org. It should look like this:

```
unsubscribe
```

Before posting a question on the 9front mailing list, please check the rest of this FQA. If asking a question possibly related to hardware, always include the output of `sysinfo(1)`!

2.2.1 – Mailing List Archives

Mailing list archives are available via 9p:

```
% 9fs 9front
post...
% ls /n/lists
/n/lists/9atom
/n/lists/9changes
/n/lists/9fans
/n/lists/9front
/n/lists/9front-commits
/n/lists/9front-fqa
/n/lists/9front-sysinfo
/n/lists/acme-sac
/n/lists/cat-v
/n/lists/cypherpunks
/n/lists/dlr
/n/lists/harvey
/n/lists/harvey-commits
/n/lists/harvey-issues
/n/lists/inferno
/n/lists/nix
/n/lists/plan9port-dev
/n/lists/sam-fans
/n/lists/sierra31
/n/lists/skunk-works
/n/lists/tscm-l
/n/lists/tuhs
/n/lists/werc
/n/lists/www-html
/n/lists/www-talk
/n/lists/www-vrml
```

Each of these directories contains messages sent to the respective mailing list in mdir format, one message per file. Erik Quanstrom's nupas upas/fs (now merged with 9front upas) can mount these directories as mailboxes, for reading directly with a mail client.

Note: Opening large mailboxes over a slow 9p link will be very slow.

2.2.2 – Other useful mailing lists

9fans — Official mailing list of Plan 9 from Bell Labs.

2.3 – Manual Pages

9front comes with extensive documentation in the form of manual pages. Considerable effort is made to make sure the man pages are up-to-date and accurate. In all cases, 1.) the source, followed by 2.) the man pages, are considered the authoritative source of information for 9front.

You can find all the 9front man pages on the web at the following sites:

http://man.9front.org

http://felloff.net/sys/man

http://man.aiju.de

http://man.cat-v.org/9front

as well as on your 9front computer.

In general, if you know the name of a command or a manual page, you can read it by executing `man command`. For example: `man vi` to read about the MIPS binary emulator. If you don't know the name of the command, or if `man command` doesn't find the manual page, you can search the manual page database by executing `lookman something`, where `something` is a likely word that might appear in the title of the manual page you're looking for. For example:

```
% lookman vesa
man 3 vga # vga(3)
man 8 realemu # realemu(8)
man 8 vga # vga(8)
```

The resulting list is presented in the form of commands that can be highlighted and sent using rio's mouse button 2 menu.

For many, having a hardcopy of the man page can be useful. To make a printable copy of a man page:

```
man -t vga realemu | lp -dstdout > vga.ps
```

or:

```
man -t vga realemu | lp -dstdout | ps2pdf > vga.pdf
```

2.3.1 – How do I display a man page source file?

The command man -w prints the location of the man page's source file:

```
% man -w vga realemu
/sys/man/3/vga
/sys/man/8/realemu
/sys/man/8/vga
```

2.3.2 – How do I write my own manual page?

As was mentioned in *FQA 0.3.2 – Man pages,* Plan 9 man pages are divided into sections based upon the features they describe. For example, the troff source of the io(1) man page is located in section 1, in the file /sys/man/1/io. You can examine this troff source for a simple example of how to format and construct a typical man page.

For additional information, read: *How to Write a Plan 9 Manual Page,* man(6), troff(1)

"I have with Plan 9 Is there a way to"

Remember: 9front developers cannot read your mind. Very detailed information is required to diagnose most serious bugs.

Also remember: It is possible you simply don't know what you're doing. If you do not understand how something is done in 9front or how it works, and can't figure out how to resolve the problem using the manual pages, *FQA 8 – Using 9front,* or *FQA 9 – Troubleshooting,* join `#9front` on `irc.freenode.net` or use the mailing list (9front@9front.org) to request help.

On the other hand, it's possible you really found a bug. If so, please file a bug report by sending an e-mail to `9front@9front.org`.

2.4.1 – Your bug report SUCKS

A minimum useful bug report contains the following:

- A complete description of what you did.

- A complete description of what you expected to happen.

- A complete description of what happened, instead.

Extra credit:

- The make and model of your computer.

- The URL returned when you run sysinfo -p on the affected system.

2.4.2 – How do I get more useful info for developers?

The following sub-sections offer some useful tips.

2.4.2.1 – Take a photo of the panic screen

Under some circumstances, you may not be able to recover text directly from a crashed system. In this situation, snap a photo of the screen, including as much of the screen in good focus as possible, and upload the image somewhere where it can be retrieved by developers.

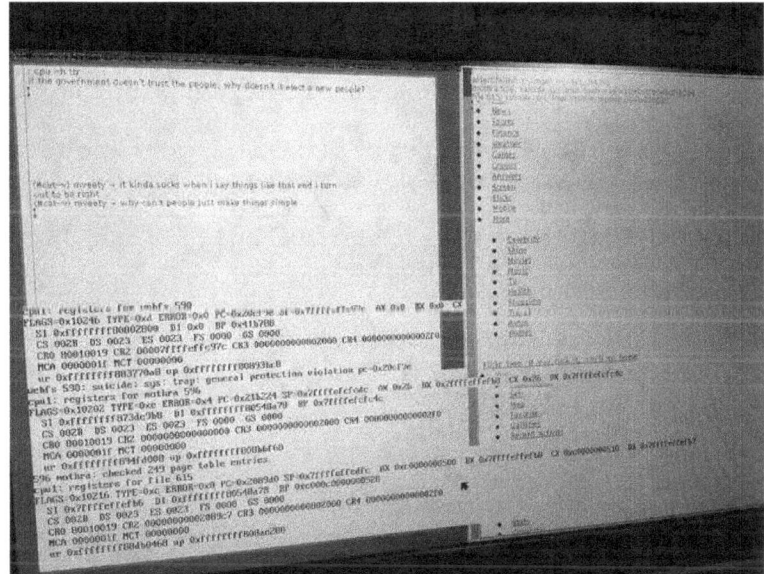

2.4.2.2 – Make a stack trace of a crashed process

```
% hget http://www.jwz.org/blog/feed | rssread
panic: D2B called on non-block c580 (double-free?)
rssread 882285: suicide: sys: trap: fault read addr=0x0 pc=0x000038ef
% acid 882285
/proc/882285/text:386 plan 9 executable
/sys/lib/acid/port
/sys/lib/acid/386
acid: lstk()
abort()+0x0 /sys/src/libc/9sys/abort.c:6
ppanic(p=0xb5a0,fmt=0xbf72)+0x146 /sys/src/libc/port/malloc.c:166
        pv=0xc100
        msg=0xc310
        v=0xdfffee90
        n=0x2b
D2B(p=0xb5a0,v=0xc580)+0x5a /sys/src/libc/port/pool.c:966
        a=0xc578
poolfreel(v=0xc580,p=0xb5a0)+0x20 /sys/src/libc/port/pool.c:1190
        ab=0xc100
poolfree(p=0xb5a0,v=0xc580)+0x41 /sys/src/libc/port/pool.c:1325
free(v=0xc588)+0x23 /sys/src/libc/port/malloc.c:250
nextxmlpull(x=0xc548)+0x334 /usr/sl/src/xmlpull/xmlpull.c:221
nextxmlpull(x=0xc548)+0x2cb /usr/sl/src/xmlpull/xmlpull.c:316
main()+0x34 /usr/sl/src/rssread/rssread.c:159
        st=0x1
        f=0xc5a8
        r=0x0
        x=0xc548
_main+0x31 /sys/src/libc/386/main9.s:16
acid:
```

2.4.2.3 – Make a process snapshot

To collect even more information than a stacktrace, you can also make a full process snapshot, which includes all the memory of the program. The snapshot file can later be analyzed (even on a different machine [even on a different machine of a different architecture]).

```
% snap 882285 > rssread.snap
```

2.5 – Sending Fixes

We take fixes.

2.5.1 – How do I write good patches? Explain the problem that your change solves. Explain why your change solves the problem well. If applicable, explain how you tested the patch, and give us a way of reproducing the issue.

Before Before making the patch, make sure your system is up to date.

Make your code match the rest of the system. Look at style(6) for a summary of our code style.

If your patch includes new features or flags, be sure to update the documentation.

If the patch is intrusive or significantly changes the design of aspects of the system, it may be worth discussing it first. Email works for this, but IRC works better.

2.5.2 – How do I send in my patches? To send changes, email 9front@9front.org with your patch attached inline. Generate the patch using

```
% bind -ac /dist/plan9front /
% cd /sys/src/your/changed/code
% git/diff . > /tmp/mypatch.diff
```

and paste the change into your email client of choice.

This project is run by hobbyists. It may take some time for people to respond. If you don't hear anything for more than a week or so, send a ping.

FQA 3 – Hardware

3.1 – Selecting Hardware

Selecting appropriate hardware to run your 9front system on is important, as it can mean the difference between success and failure of a project. Fortunately, most common PC hardware is at least minimally functional in Plan 9 (excluding certain exotic audio, VGA, and WiFi devices). Nowadays, thanks to 9boot(8), realemu(8), and the VESA driver, it is at least very likely that your PC will boot. In addition, most popular virtualization platforms are reasonably well supported.

Check *FQA 3.2 – Known Working Hardware* as well as the various supported hardware pages on the Bell Labs Plan 9 wiki to help determine if your hardware or VM is supported.

3.2 – Known Working Hardware

This list adds to the various supported hardware pages on the Plan 9 from Bell Labs wiki. **Note:** NONE of these lists are all-inclusive. Some drivers listed on the Bell Labs wiki have not been tested by 9front developers. The following list consists of hardware, 1.) that we have actually used, or 2.) about which we have received reliable reports from users.

Some drivers and their options are also documented in plan9.ini(8).

Read: *FQA 1.3.1.2 – New Hardware Support* for information about hardware drivers that are new in 9front.

3.2.0 – Input Devices

3.2.0.1 – Mice

Almost any PS/2 or USB mouse is going to work. The following are preferred for use with Plan 9.

3.2.0.1.1 – IBM/Lenovo

N700 Wireless/Bluetooth, 3 button Mouse and Laser Pointer

Part Number: 888015450
DPI: 1200
"Just works" with USB receiver. No additional driver required.

ScrollPoint Optical Mouse, 3 button, USB/PS2

Part Number: 31P7405
DPI: 800

3.2.0.2 – Keyboards

Almost any AT, PS/2, or USB keyboard is going to work. The following are preferred for use with Plan 9.

3.2.0.2.1 – IBM/Lenovo

IBM Model M 1391401
Part Number: 1391401

IBM UltraNav SK–8835
Part Number: SK–8835

3.2.0.2.2 – TEX Electronics

TEX Shinobi

3.2.1 – Audio Audio support is much improved in 9front, with added support for AC97, Intel HDA, and (ha!) Soundblaster 16.

AMD FCH Azalia Controller
vid/did: 1022/780d

Intel 888 Microsoft UAA bus for HD audio
vid/did: 8086/284b

Intel 82801CA/CAM AC97
vid/did: 8086/2485

Intel 82801 DB DBM/DA AC 97
vid/did: 8086/24c5

Intel 486486 82801IB/IR/IH HD Audio
vid/did: 8086/293e

Intel Gemeni Lake
vid/did 8086/3198

Intel HD NM10/ICH7
vid/did: 8086/27d8

Intel HD 6 Series/C200 Series
vid/did: 8086/1c20

Intel HD 7 Series/C210 Series
vid/did: 8086/1e20

3.2.2 – Graphics Many video cards for which there exists no native VGA driver can be made to work with the generic VESA driver. Examples are provided below.

3.2.2.1 – AGP

NVidia GeForce FX 5200 128MB VGA output
```
vid/did: 10de/0322
monitor=vesa vgasize=1600x1200x32
monitor=dellst2210 vgasize=1920x1080x32
```

NVidia GeForce FX 5700
```
vid/did: 10de/0341
monitor=vesa vgasize=1600x1200x32
monitor=dellst2210 vgasize=1920x1080x32
```

3.2.2.2 – Integrated

ATI Mobility Radeon 7500 128MB DVI/VGA output
```
vid/did: 1002/4c57
monitor=vesa vgasize=1024x768x32
```

ATI Mobility Radeon FireGL V3200/X600
```
vid/did: 1002/3154
monitor=vesa vgasize=1600x1200x32
```

ATI RS880
```
monitor=vesa vgasize=1280x1024x32
```

ATI X1300

Intel Mobile 945GM/GMS/GME, 943/940GML Express
```
vid/did: 8086/27a6
monitor=vesa vgasize=1400x1050x32
monitor=x60t vgasize=1400x1050x32
```

Intel X3100/GM965/PM965/GL960
```
vid/did: 8086/2a03
monitor=vesa vgasize=1680x1050x32
```

Intel Mobile Intel 4 Series 4500MHD
```
vid/did: 8086/2a42, 8086/2a43
monitor=vesa vgasize=1440x900x32
monitor=x301 vgasize=1440x900x32
```

Intel HD 3rd Gen Core processor Graphics Controller
```
vid/did: 8086/0166
monitor-vesa vgasize=1366x768x32
monitor-x230 vgasize-1366x768x32
```

NVidia GeForce FX Go5200 64M
```
vid/did: 10de/0324
monitor=cinema vgasize=1152x768x32
```

S3 SuperSavage IX/C 16MB

```
vid/did: 5333/8c2e
monitor=t23 vgasize=1024x768x32
monitor=vesa vgasize=1024x768x32
```

3.2.2.3 – PCI Express

NVidia GeForce 6200 AGB

```
vid/did: 10de/0220
```

NVidia GeForce 6200 LE

```
vid/did: 10de/0163
monitor=e228wfp vgasize=1680x1050x32
```

NVidia GeForce 8400 GS

```
vid/did: 10de/0422
monitor=vesa vgasize=1680x1050x32
```

NVidia GeForce 8600 GT

```
vid/did: 10de/0402
monitor=vesa vgasize=1600x1200x32
```

NVidia GeForce GTX 550

```
vid/did: 10de/0bee
monitor=vesa vgasize=1600x1200x32
```

3.2.3 – Networking

3.2.3.1 – Ethernet

Ethernet is well supported across many vendors and chipsets. 9front introduces a "medium-to-low quality" driver for Broadcom BCM57xx cards, previously unsupported by Plan 9.

3.2.3.1.1 – Integrated

Broadcom BCM5751M NetXtreme Gigabit

```
vid/did: 14e4/167d
tested 100/1000 mbps
```

Broadcom BCM5755/5780 NetXtreme Gigabit
> vid/did: 14e4/167b
> tested 100/1000 mbps

Broadcom BCM5782 NetXtreme Gigabit
> vid/did: 14e4/1696

Intel X553/X550-AT 10GBASE-T
> vid/did: 8086/15c8

Intel 82540EP Gigabit
> vid/did: 8086/101e
> tested 100/1000 mbps

Intel 82562ET
> tested 10/100 mbps

Intel 82566MM Gigabit
> vid/did: 8086/1049
> tested 100/1000 mbps

Intel 82567LM 82567LM-2 Gigabit
> vid/did: 8086/10f5
> tested 100/1000 mbps

Intel 82573L Gigabit
> vid/did: 8086/109a
> tested: 100/1000 mbps

Intel 82579LM Gigabit
> vid/did: 8086/1502
> tested: 100/1000 mbps

Intel 82801CAM PRO/100 VE
> vid/did: 8086/1031
> tested 10/100 mbps

Realtek RTL8139

vid/did: 10ec/8139
tested 10/100/1000 mbps

Realtek RTL8169/RTL8101E/RTL8102E

vid/did: 10ec/8136
tested 10/100/1000 mbps

3.2.3.1.2 – USB

Beceem Communications CLEAR Stick

vid/did 198f:8160
This is a WiMAX device that appears as a USB CDC Ethernet device
Works with nusb/ether

RNDIS

Android phones should work
Works with nusb/ether

3.2.3.1.3 – PCMCIA

3Com 3c589c

Set the following in `plan9.ini`: `irq=3 port=0x300`

3.2.3.2 – WiFi

9front adds support for several WiFi adapters from Ralink and Intel, as well as support for WPA and WPA2.

Read: wpa(8), and `plan9.ini`(8)

3.2.3.2.1 – Bridge (external)

Iogear GWU627

802.11n
connect ethernet port to GWU627
HTTP management interface requires Javascript. Managed to program it using Inferno's `charon` browser, which supports ecmascript 1.0.

Vonets VAP11G

802.11g
connect ethernet port to VAP11G
Requires a proprietary Windows program (ships with the device) to program its settings before using it for the first time.

3.2.3.2.2 – Mini-PCI

Actiontec 800MIP

802.11b
often branded Lucent WaveLAN
```
ether0=type=wavelanpci ssid=MESH station=T42 irq=11
```

Ralink RT2860 802.11b

3.2.3.2.3 – Mini-PCI Express

Intel Centrino Advanced-N 6205 Taylor Peak (iwl-6005)

vid/did: 8086/0085
802.11g
```
ether0=type=iwl essid=MESH
```

Intel Centrino Ultimate-N (iwl 6000)

802.11g
```
ether0=type=iwl essid=MESH
```

Intel Centrino Wireless-N 100

802.11g
```
ether0=type=iwl essid=MESH
```

Intel Centrino Wireless-N 2230

802.11g
```
ether0=type=iwl essid=MESH
```

Intel PRO Wireless 3945ABG (wpi-3945abg)

802.11g
```
ether0=type=wpi essid=MESH
```

Intel WiFi Link 1000/4965/5100/5300/5350 AGN

```
802.11g
ether0=type=iwl essid=MESH
```

Intel Wireless AC 8260/8265

```
802.11g
ether0=type=iwl essid=MESH
```

Intel Wireless AC 9260

```
802.11g
ether0=type=iwl essid=MESH
```

Ralink RT3090

```
802.11g
```

3.2.3.2.4 – PCI

Ralink RT3090

```
802.11b
```

3.2.3.2.5 – PCMCIA

Linksys WPC11

```
802.11b
Prism 2.5
ISL37300P
RevA
```

Lucent WaveLAN PC24E-H-FC

```
802.11b
ether0=type=wavelan essid=MESH crypt=off station=x61 irq=11
```

3.2.4 – Tablet Digitizers

Support for Wacom serial tablets was added in 2012. The touchscreen digitizers in some Lenovo ThinkPads (notably, the X230) also seem to function without need of any drivers (presumably, controlled by the BIOS).

3.2.4.1 – Serial

3.2.4.1.1 – Integrated

Wacom WACF004
ThinkPad X4* series tablets

To enable the tablet's serial port in `plan9.ini`:
```
uart2=type=isa port=0x200 irq=5
```
To turn on the tablet:
```
aux/wacom; aux/tablet &
```

Wacom WACF008
ThinkPad X6* series tablets

To enable the tablet's serial port in `plan9.ini`:
```
uart2=type=isa port=0x200 irq=5
```
To turn on the tablet:
```
aux/wacom; aux/tablet &
```

3.2.4.2 – USB

3.2.4.2.1 – Integrated

Wacom (from ThinkPad X230 Tablet, model unknown)

Treated as a mouse.

3.2.4.2.2 – External

Wacom CTE–640

Treated as a mouse.

3.2.5 – Laptops

3.2.5.1 – Acer

Aspire 5100 (donated by some poor kid)

cpu: 1795MHz AuthenticAMD AMD–K8, works
ethernet: rtl8139 100Mbps, works
keyboard and touchpad, works
graphics: RS482M ATI RADEON Xpress Series,
`monitor=vesa vgasize=1024x768x32` (native resolution not in VESA BIOS); radeon driver untested
wifi: Atheros AR5005G, does not work
audio: SB450 High Definition Audio Controller

3.2.5.2 – IBM/Lenovo

3.2.5.2.1 – ThinkPad ThinkPads are the best supported laptops in 9front because Think-Pads are what the developers use.

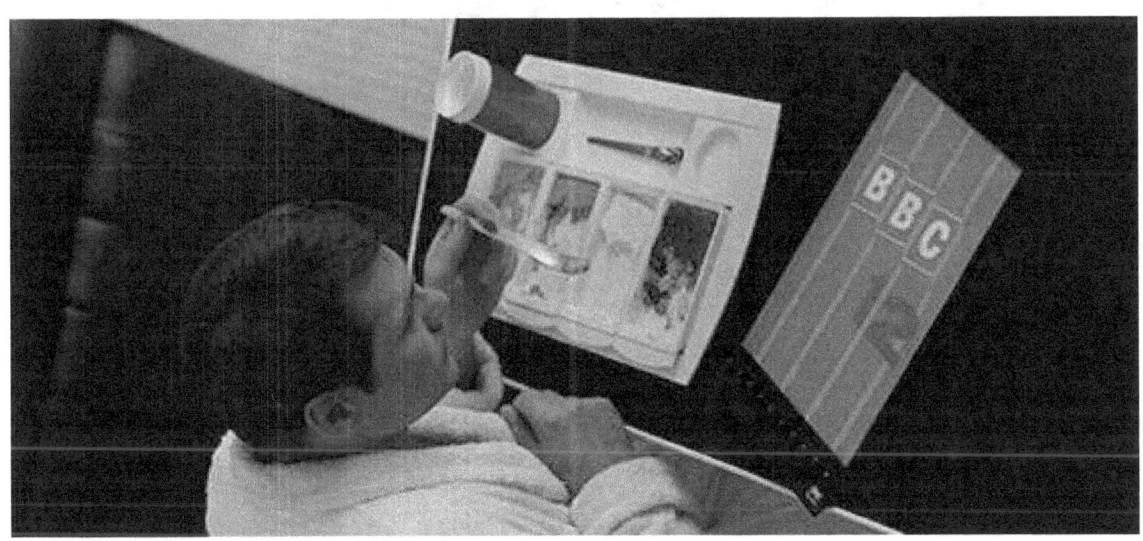

380D

2635–3AU

    cpu: cpu0: 152MHz GenuineIntel P55C MMX (AX 00000543 CX 00000000 DX
    008001BF)
    graphics: Neomagic MagicGraph 128ZV
    monitor=vga vgasize=800x600x16

ethernet: 3Com 3C589 PCMCIA, works

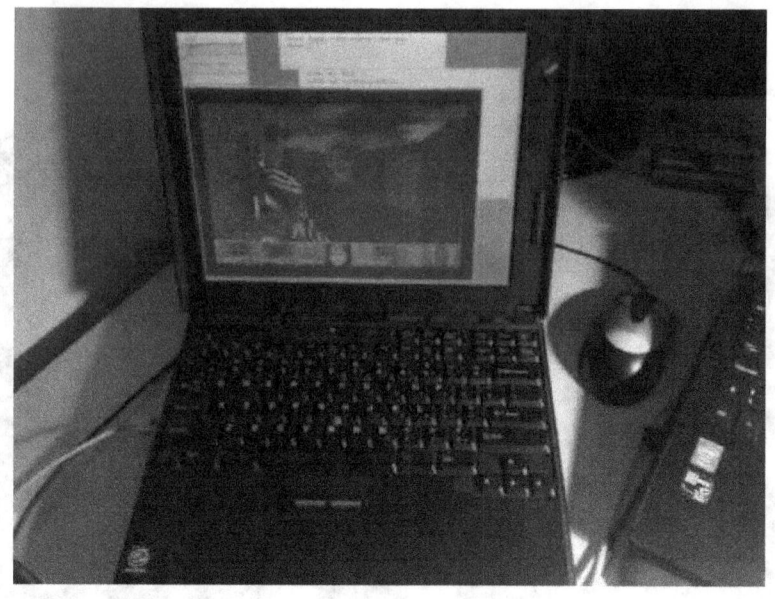

G50

nnnn–nnn

cpu: 2394MHz GenuineIntel P6, cpuid: AX 00040651 CX 77DAFBBF DX BFEBFBFF
graphics: Intel Corporation Haswell-ULT Integrated Graphics Controller,
`realemu(8) monitor=vesa vgasize=1366x768x32`
ethernet: Realtek Semiconductor Co., Ltd. RTL8111/8168/8411 PCI Express Gigabit
Ethernet Controller, works
audio: Intel Corporation Haswell-ULT HD Audio Controller, works
usb: Intel Corporation 8 Series USB EHCI #1, works

R400

7439–1DG

cpu: 2527MHz GenuineIntel Core 2/Xeon, cpuid: AX 0x10676 CX 0x8E3FD DX
0xBFEBFBFF
graphics: Mobile Intel GM45 Express/4500MHD,
`realemu(8) monitor=vesa vgasize=1440x900x32`
ethernet: Intel 82567LM 82567LM-2 Gigabit (10/100/1000), works
wifi: Intel WiFi Link 5100 AGN Mini-PCI Express, works
disk controller: Intel ICH9M/ME ICH9M/ME AHCI, works
dvd: MATSHITADVD-RAM UJ870A SB04 HE34 068E34 068597, works
audio: Intel 486486 82801IB/IR/IH HD Audio, works
usb: works
mp: mp + sata, ethernet works with `*acpi=1`

T23

2647-HSU

cpu: Intel Mobile Pentium III-M 866 MHz, 1.2 GHz
graphics: S3 SuperSavage IX/C 16MB, VGA 1024x768x32,
`realemu(8) monitor=vesa vgasize=1024x768x32`
ethernet: Intel 82801CAM PRO/100 VE or Intel 82562ET (10/100), works
wifi: Actiontec 800MIP (branded Lucent WaveLAN) Mini-PCI, works
audio: AC97, works

T42

2373-BK4

cpu: Intel Pentium M (Dothan) 1.7 GHz
graphics: ATI Mobility Radeon 7500 32MB,
`realemu(8) monitor=vesa vgasize=1024x768x32`
ethernet: Intel Gigabit Ethernet (10/100/1000), works
wifi: IBM 11a/b/g Mini-PCI, does not work; replaced with Actiontec 800MIP
(branded Lucent WaveLAN) Mini-PCI, works
disk controller: 82801DBM (ICH4-M), IDE DMA works
audio: AC97, works

T43p

2669-A92

cpu: Intel Pentium M (Dothan) 2.0 GHz (cpuid: AX 0x06D8 CX 0x0180 DX
0xAFE9FBFF)
graphics: ATI Mobility Radeon FireGL V3200/X600,
`realemu(8) monitor=vesa vgasize=1600x1200x32` with internal LCD
ethernet: Broadcom BCM5751M (10/100/1000), works
wifi: replaced with Vonets VAP11G, works
disk controller: Intel 82801FBM SATA AHCI (ICH6-M): untested
usb: works
scram works with `*acpi=1`
mouse button 2 works with trackpad disabled in BIOS
aux/acpi: works

T60p

2007-94U

cpu: Intel Core Duo (Yonah) 2.16GHz (cpuid: AX 0x06E8 CX 0xC1A9 DX
0xBFE9FBFF)
graphics: ATI MOBILITY FireGL V5200
`realemu(8) monitor=vesa vgasize-1600x1200x32` with internal LCD
audio: Intel BA101897 IDT High Definition, untested
ethernet: Intel 82573L Intel PRO/1000 PL (10/100/1000), works
wifi: Intel PRO Wireless 3945ABG (wpi-3945abg), may work now with `wpi` driver
disk controller: Intel 82801GB/GBM PATA100, 82801GBM/GHM AHCI, works
usb: works

mp: mp + sata, ethernet, usb works with *acpi=
mouse button 2 works with trackpad disabled in BIOS

8741-C4G

cpu: Intel Core 2 Duo (Merom) 2.33 GHz (cpuid: AX 0x06F6 CX 0xE3BD DX 0xBFEBFBFF)
graphics: ATI MOBILITY FireGL V5250, realemu(8) monitor=vesa vgasize=1400x1050x32 (native 1680x1050 resolution not in VESA BIOS); radeon driver does not work
audio: Intel HDA NM10/ICH7, works
ethernet: Intel 82573L Gigabit Ethernet (10/100/1000), works
wifi: Intel PRO Wireless 3945ABG (wpi-3945abg), works with wpi driver
disk controller: Intel 82801GBM/GHM (ICH7-M) SATA AHCI, works
usb: works

T61

7659-CTO

cpu: Intel Core 2 Duo (Merom) 2.0 GHz FSB, 2-4MB L2 Cache CPU
graphics: Intel GMA X3100,
realemu(8) monitor=vesa vgasize=1280x800x32 with internal LCD; monitor=vesa vgasize=1680x1050x32 with VGA or Mini Doc DVI output and external monitor
ethernet: Intel 82566MM (10/100/1000), works
wifi: Intel Wireless WiFi Link 4965 AGN Mini-PCI Express, should work with iwl driver
disk controller: Intel 82801HBM/HEM PATA, Intel 82801HBM SATA AHCI (ICH8-M): IDE DMA works, SATA works
usb: works
mp: mp + sata, ethernet, usb works with *acpi=
mouse button 2 works with trackpad disabled in BIOS

7661-12U

cpu: Intel Core 2 Duo (Merom) 2.0 GHz FSB, 2-4MB L2 Cache CPU
graphics: Intel GMA X3100,
realemu(8) monitor=vesa vgasize=1280x800x32 with internal LCD; monitor=vesa vgasize=1680x1050x32 with VGA or Mini Doc DVI output and external monitor
ethernet: Intel 82566MM (10/100/1000), works
wifi: Intel PRO Wireless 3945ABG (wpi-3945abg), may work now with wpi driver; replaced with Wavelan PC24E-H-FC PCMCIA, works
disk controller: Intel 82801HBM/HEM PATA, Intel 82801HBM SATA AHCI (ICH8-M): IDE DMA works, SATA works
usb: works
mp: mp + sata, ethernet, usb works with *acpi=
mouse button 2 works with trackpad disabled in BIOS

T400

6475-EC7

cpu: 2261MHz GenuineIntel Core 2/Xeon (cpuid: AX 0x10676 CX 0x8E3FD DX 0xBFEBFBFF)
graphics: Intel Corporation Mobile 4 Series,
`realemu(8) monitor=vesa vgasize=1440x900x32` with internal LCD
ethernet: i82567: 1000Mbps, works
wifi: Intel WiFi Link 5100 AGN Mini-PCI Express, works
disk controller: Intel ICH9M/ME AHCI, works
audio: Intel HDA, should work

T410i

2518-4QG

cpu: Intel(R) Core(TM) i5 CPU M 430 @ 2.27GHz
graphics: Intel Graphics Media Accelerator HD,
`realemu(8) monitor=vesa vgasize=1280x800x32` with internal LCD
ethernet: Intel 82577LM Gigabit, works
wifi: unknown, reportedly works
audio: unknown, reportedly works

T420s

4171-53U

cpu: Intel® Core™ i5-2540M (2.6GHz, 3MB L3, 1333MHz FSB) (cpuid: AX 000206A7 CX 17BAE3FF DX BFEBFBFF)
graphics: Intel HD Graphics 3000 (integrated Sandy Bridge GPU),
`realemu(8) monitor-vesa vgasize=1600x900x32`
ethernet: Intel 82579LM Gigabit, works
audio: Intel HD 6 Series/C200 Series, works
wifi: Intel Centrino Advanced-N 6205 Taylor Peak, etheriwl (firmware: iwn-6005), works

T430s

2353-ABU

T431s

20AA-000BUS

cpu: 1796MHz GenuineIntel P6 (cpuid: AX 000306A9 CX 77BAE3BF DX BFEBFBFF)
graphics: Intel 3rd Gen Core processor Graphics Controller,
`realemu(8) monitor=vesa vgasize=1920x1080x32` with third party Samsung internal LCD
audio: 7 Series/C210 Series HDA Controller, works
ethernet: Intel 82579LM (10/100/1000), works
wifi: Intel Centrino Advanced-N 6235, works
disk controller: Intel 7 Series Chipset Family 6-port SATA Controller [AHCI mode], works
usb: works
scram works with `*acpi=`
mouse button 2 works with trackpad disabled in BIOS

W500

4061-BM8

cpu: Intel Core 2 Duo (Penryn) 2.53 GHz (cpuid: AX 0x1067A CX 0x0408E3FD DX 0xBFEBFBFF)

graphics: Intel GMA 4500MHD + ATI Mobility Radeon HD3650 (switched off in BIOS), realemu(8) monitor=vesa vgasize=1920x1200x32; monitor=auto vgasize=1920x1200x32

ethernet: Intel 82567LM Gigabit Ethernet (10/100/1000), works

wifi: Intel Ultimate-N 5300 AGN (iwn-5000), works

disk controller: Intel 82801IBM/IEM (ICH9M/ICH9M-E) SATA AHCI, works

audio: Intel HDA 82801I, works

usb: works

ssd: Samsung SSD 850 EVO 500GB EMT02B6Q S2RBNX0HA34127X, works

W520

4260-A47

cpu: Intel Core i7-2760QM (Sandy Bridge) 2.4 GHz (cpuid: AX 0x206A7 CX 0x17BAE3FF DX 0xBFEBFBFF)

graphics: Intel HD 3000 + NVIDIA Quadro 1000M (switched off in BIOS), realemu(8) monitor=vesa vgasize=1920x1080x32; monitor=auto vgasize=1920x1080x32 (on 50 Hz)

ethernet: Intel 82579LM Gigabit Ethernet (10/100/1000), works

wifi: Intel Advanced-N 6205 AGN (iwn 6005), works

disk controller: Intel 6 Series/C200 SATA AHCI, works

audio: Intel 6 Series/C200 HDA, works

usb: works

X1 Tablet (1st Gen)

cpu: Intel Xeon E3-1200 v5/E3-1500 v5
graphics: Intel HD Graphics 515,
`realemu(8) monitor=vesa vgasize=2160x1440x32`
tablet: doesn't work
wifi: Intel 8260 (iwm-8000C-34 firmware), works
audio: Intel Sunrise Point-LP HD Audio, works

X41 tablet

cpu: Intel Pentium M (Dothan) 1.6GHz LV (778) L2 2 MB cache
graphics: Intel GMA900,
`realemu(8) monitor=vesa vgasize=1024x768x32`
tablet: WACF004, works
ethernet: BCM5751M (10/100/1000), works
wifi: Intel PRO/Wireless 2915ABG Mini-PCI, does not work

X60s

1704-GL5

coreboot
cpu: cpu0: 1663MHz GenuineIntel P6 (cpuid: AX 0x06E8 CX 0xC1A9 DX 0xBFE9FBFF)
graphics: Intel 945GM,
`realemu(8) monitor=vesa vgasize=1024x768x16`
ethernet: Intel 82573L Intel PRO/1000 PL, works
audio: Intel HDA, untested
wifi: Ralink RT3090, works

X60 Tablet

6363-CTO

cpu: Intel Core Duo (Yonah) L2400 LV 1.66 GHz (2MB Cache) cpu0: 1663MHz GenuineIntel P6 (AX 000006EC CX 0000C1A9 DX BFE9FBFF)

lcd: replaced with HV121P01-100 (1400x1050)

graphics: Intel Graphics Media Accelerator 950,

`realemu(8)` `monitor=x60t vgasize=1400x1050x32;` `monitor=vesa vgasize=1280x1024x32` (native 1400x1050 resolution not in VESA BIOS)

tablet: WACF008, works

ethernet: Intel 82573L (10/100/1000), works

audio: Intel HD Audio with AD1981HD codec, speaker and green lineout work with `echo pin 5,3 >/dev/audioctl`

wifi: Intel WiFi Link 5100 AGN, works — flashed with custom BIOS to remove WiFi card whitelist

disk controller: Intel 82801GBM/GHM (ICH7-M Family) SATA Controller [AHCI mode], untested

mp: mp + sata, ethernet works with *acpi

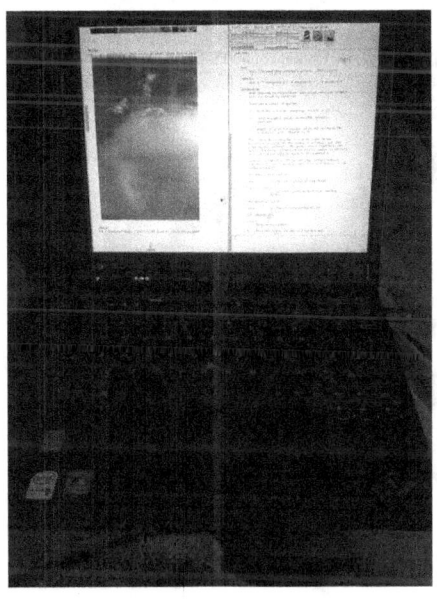

X61s

cpu: Intel Core 2 Duo

graphics: Intel GM965/GL960,

`realemu(8) monitor=vesa vgasize=1024x768x32`

ethernet: Intel 82566MM (10/100/1000), works

wifi: Intel PRO/Wireless 4965 AG or AGN '[Kedron]' Mini-PCI Express, untested, should work with `iwl` driver

disk controller: Intel 82801HBM SATA (ICH8-M): IDE DMA works, SATA works

mp: mp + sata, ethernet works with `*acpi=`

X61 Tablet

7767–01U

cpu: Intel Core 2 Duo CPU L7700 (1.80 GHz)
lcd: replaced with HV121P01–100 (1400x1050)
graphics: Intel GMA X3100,
`realemu(8)` `monitor=x60t vgasize=1400x1050x32;` `monitor=vesa vgasize=1280x1024x32` (native 1400x1050 resolution not in VESA BIOS)
tablet: WACF008, works
ethernet: Intel 82566MM (10/100/1000), works
audio: Intel HDA, works
wifi: Intel Centrino Advanced-N 6205 Taylor Peak (iwl-6005), works — flashed with custom BIOS to remove WiFi card whitelist
disk controller: Intel 82801HBM SATA (ICH8–M): IDE DMA works, SATA works mp: mp + sata, ethernet works with `*acpi=`

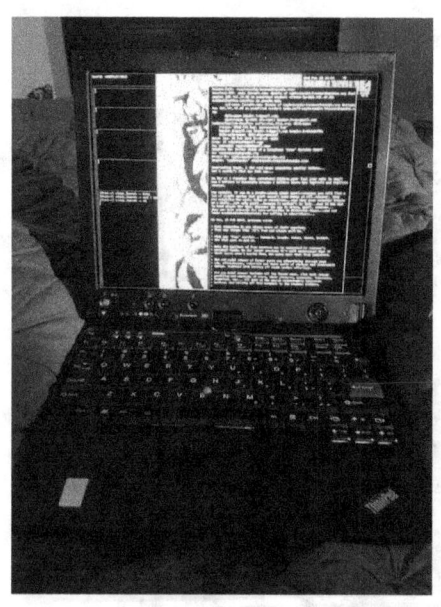

X131e

3368–2FU

cpu: 1397MHz GenuineIntel P6 (cpuid: AX 0x206A7 CX 0x15BAE3BF DX 0xBFEBF-BFF)
graphics: Intel HD Graphics 3000,
`realemu(8) monitor=vesa vgasize=1366x768x32`
ethernet: Realtek RTL8167 PCIe Gigabit Ethernet: works
audio: Intel HDA, works

6283-22U

cpu: 1397MHz GenuineIntel P6 (cpuid: AX 0x206A7 CX 0x15BAE3BF DX 0xBFEBF-BFF)
graphics: Intel HD Graphics 3000,
realemu(8) monitor=vesa vgasize=1366x768x32
ethernet: Realtek RTL8167 PCIe Gigabit Ethernet: works
wifi: Intel Centrino Advanced-N 6205: works
audio: Intel HDA, works

X200

7455-A54

cpu: Intel Core 2 Duo
graphics: Mobile Intel GMA 4500MHD,
realemu(8) monitor=vesa vgasize=1280x800x32
ethernet: Intel 82567LF Gigabit (10/100/1000), works
wifi: Intel WiFi Link 5150, works
disk controller: Intel ICH9M/ME ICH9M/ME AHCI, works
audio: Intel 486486 82801IB/IR/IH HD Audio, works
usb: works

X200s

7466-3SG

cpu: 1862MHz GenuineIntel Core 2/Xeon (cpuid: AX 0x1067b CX 0x8E3FD DX 0xBFEBFBFF)
graphics: Mobile Intel GM45 Express/4500,
realemu(8) monitor=vesa vgasize=1280x800x32
ethernet: Intel 82567LM 82567LM-2 Gigabit (10/100/1000), works
wifi: Intel WiFi Link 5300 AGN Mini-PCI Express, works

disk controller: Intel ICH9M/ME ICH9M/ME AHCI, works
audio: Intel 486486 82801IB/IR/IH HD Audio, works
usb: works
mp: mp + sata, ethernet works with `*acpi=1`

X201

3323-DBG

cpu: 2661MHz GenuineIntel P6
graphics: Mobile Intel GMA 5700MHD,
`realemu(8) monitor=vesa vgasize=1280x800x32`
ethernet: Intel Corporation 82577LM Intel 82577LM Gigabit, works
wifi: Intel Centrino Ultimate-N 6300 AGN, works
disk controller: Intel Corporation PCH (Ibex Peak) SATA AHCI, works
audio: Intel HDA, works
ssd: INTEL SSDSC2BW180A3L, works
usb: works

X220

4291-4CG

cpu: 2791MHz GenuineIntel P6 (cpuid: AX 0x206A7 CX 0x17BAE3FF DX 0xBFEBF-BFF)
graphics: Intel HD 3000,
`realemu(8) monitor=vesa vgasize=1366x768x32`
ethernet: Intel 82579 (10/100/1000), works
audio: Intel HDA, works
wifi: Intel Centrino Advanced-N 6205, works
disk controller: works
ssd: INTEL SSDSA2BW160G3, works
usb: works
aux/acpi: works

The IBM chiclet keyboard.

X230

2306-CTO

cpu: Intel Core i5-3320M (2.60 GHz, 3MB L3, 1600MHz FSB), cpuid: AX 0x306A9 CX 0x77BAE3FF DX 0xBFEBFBFF

graphics: Intel HD 3rd Gen Core processor Graphics Controller,
```
realemu(8)              monitor=x230 vgasize=1366x768x32;
monitor=vesa vgasize=1366x768x32
```

ethernet: Intel 82579LM Gigabit (10/100/1000), works

wifi: Intel Centrino Advanced-N 6205 Taylor Peak, etheriwl (firmware: iwn-6005), works

disk controller: Intel 7 Series Chipset Family 6-port SATA Controller AHCI mode, ahci, works

usb: Intel 7 Series/C210 Series Chipset Family USB Enhanced Host Controller #1, ehci, works

audio: Intel 7 Series/C210 Series Chipset Family High Definition Audio Controller, works

efi: works

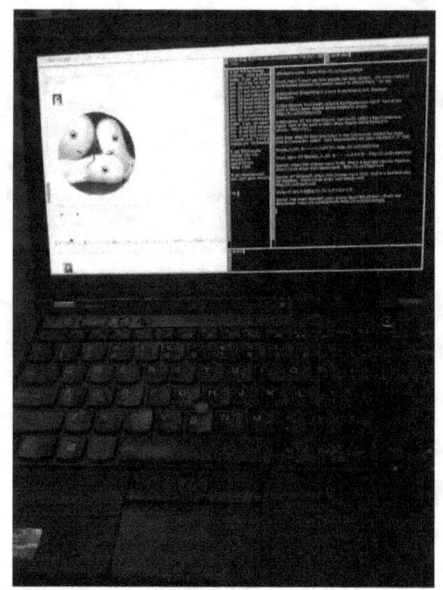

X230 Tablet

3434-CTO

    cpu: Intel Core i5-3320M (Ivy Bridge), 2.6 GHz, 3 MB Shared L3 Cache, 2C/4T, 35 W TDP, 22 nm (cpuid: AX 0x306A9 CX 0x77BAE3FF DX 0xBFEBFBFF)
    graphics: Intel HD 4000,
    `realemu(8) monitor=vesa vgasize=1366x768x32`
    tablet: Wacom USB internal, works
    ethernet: Intel 82579 (10/100/1000), works
    audio: Intel HDA, works
    wifi: Intel 802.11b/g/n, might work
    disk controller: works
    ssd: SAMSUNG SSD 830 Series CXM03B1Q S0XYNEAC774074 128GB, works
    usb: disable USB3 in BIOS, works
    aux/acpi: battery works

X230 Tablet

3434-DB7

    cpu: Intel(R) Core(TM) i7-3520M CPU @ 2.90GHz (cpuid: AX 000306A9 CX 77BAE3FF DX BFEBFBFF)
    graphics: Intel HD 4000,
    `realemu(8) monitor=vesa vgasize=1366x768x32`
    tablet: Wacom USB internal, works
    ethernet: Intel 82579 (10/100/1000), works
    audio: Intel HDA, works
    wifi: Intel Centrino Advanced-N 6205, works
    disk controller: works
    ssd: LITEONIT LCS-128M6S DC72205 S0C41178Z1ZSVB159894 128GB, works
    usb: disable USB3 in BIOS, works
    aux/acpi: battery works

X240

20AL-CTO

wifi: Intel Wireless-N 7260, does not work, but may not be hard to add to existing etheriwl driver

X250

20CM-CTO

    cpu: Intel(R) Core(TM) i5-5200U CPU @ 2.20GHz, cpuid: AX 000306D4 CX 77FAF-BBF DX BFEBFBFF

    graphics: Intel Corporation Broadwell-U Integrated Graphics,

    `realemu(8) monitor=vesa vgasize=1920x1080x32`

    ethernet: Intel Corporation Ethernet Connection (3) I218-LM (10/100/1000), works

    wifi: Intel Wireless-N 7265, does not work, but may not be hard to add to existing etheriwl driver

    disk controller: Intel Corporation Wildcat Point-LP SATA Controller [AHCI Mode], works

    usb: Intel Corporation Wildcat Point-LP USB EHCI Controller, works

    audio: Intel Corporation Broadwell-U Audio Controller, works

    aux/acpi: works

20CM-CTO1WW

    cpu: Intel(R) Core(TM) i5-5200U CPU @ 2.20GHz, cpuid: AX 000306D4 CX 77FAF-BBF DX BFEBFBFF

    graphics: Intel Corporation Broadwell-U Integrated Graphics,

    `realemu(8) monitor=vesa vgasize=1920x1080x32`

    ethernet: Intel Corporation Ethernet Connection (3) I218-LM (10/100/1000), works

    wifi: Intel Wireless-N 7265, does not work, but may not be hard to add to existing etheriwl driver

    disk controller: Intel Corporation Wildcat Point-LP SATA Controller [AHCI Mode], works

    usb: Intel Corporation Wildcat Point-LP USB EHCI Controller, works

    audio: Intel Corporation Broadwell-U Audio Controller, works

    aux/acpi: works

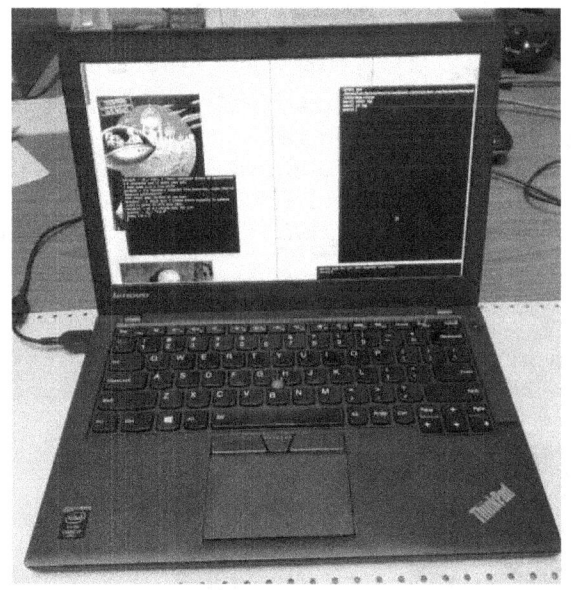

X260

nnnn-nnn

cpu: 2496MHz GenuineIntel P6, cpuid: AX 000406E3 CX 77FAFBFF DX BFEBFBFF
graphics: Intel Corporation HD Graphics 520,
`realemu(8) monitor=vesa vgasize=1920x1080x32`
ethernet: Intel Corporation Ethernet Connection I219-LM (10/100/1000), works
wifi: Intel Corporation Centrino Advanced-N 6235, works with etheriwl driver
disk controller: Intel Corporation Sunrise Point-LP SATA Controller [AHCI mode], works
usb: Intel Corporation Sunrise Point-LP USB 3.0 xHCI Controller, works
audio: Intel Corporation Sunrise Point-LP HD Audio, works
aux/acpi: works

X301

2776-P4U

cpu: Intel Core 2 Duo SU9400 1.4GHz 3MB cache, cpuid: AX 0x1067A CX 0x408E3FD DX 0xBFEBFBFF
graphics: Mobile Intel GM45 Express/4500MHD,
`realemu(8)        monitor=x301 vgasize=1440x900x32;`
`monitor=vesa vgasize=1440x900x32`
ethernet: Intel 82567LM 82567LM-2 Gigabit (10/100/1000), works
wifi: Intel WiFi Link 5100 AGN Mini-PCI Express, works
disk controller: Intel ICH9M/ME ICH9M/ME AHCI, works
ssd: Samsung MMCRE64G8MPP-0VA 64GB, works
dvd: Matsushita DVD-RAM UJ-844, works
audio: Intel HD 486486 82801IB/IR/IH, works
usb: works
mp: mp + sata, ethernet works with `*acpi=1`

2776-P6U

cpu: Intel Core 2 Duo SU9400 1.4GHz 3MB cache, cpuid: AX 00010676 CX 0008E3FD DX BFEBFBFF
graphics: Mobile Intel GM45 Express/4500MHD,
`realemu(8)` `monitor=x301 vgasize=1440x900x32;`
`monitor=vesa vgasize=1440x900x32`
ethernet: Intel 82567LM Gigabit (10/100/1000), works
wifi: Intel WiFi Link 5100 AGN Mini-PCI Express, works
disk controller: 82801IBM/IEM (ICH9M/ICH9M-E) 4 port SATA Controller AHCI mode, works
audio: Intel HD 82801I (ICH9 Family), works
usb: works
mp: mp + sata, ethernet works with `*acpi=1`

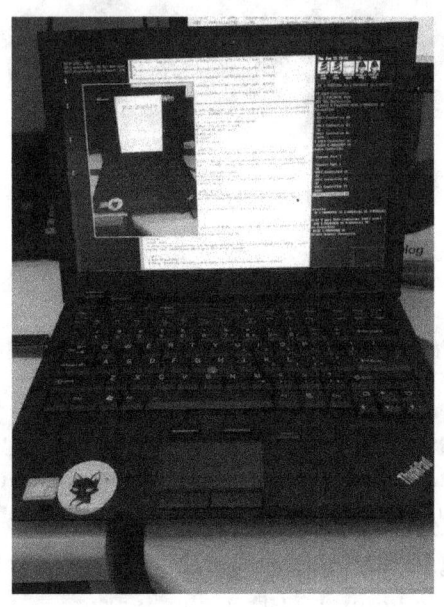

Yoga 370

20JH-002AUS

cpu: 2712MHz GenuineIntel P6, cpuid: AX 000806E9 CX 77FAFBFF DX BFEBFBFF
graphics: Intel Corporation Skylake Gaussian Mixture Model,
`realemu(8) monitor=vesa vgasize=1920x1080x32`
ethernet: Intel I219-LM Gigabit (10/100/1000), works with dongle
wifi: Intel 8265, does not work
audio: does not seem to work

3.2.5.3 – Toshiba

3.2.5.3.1 – Satellite

M30–S309

cpu: 1397MHz GenuineIntel P6 (AX 00000695 CX 00000180 DX A7E9F9BF)
graphics: NVidia GeForce FX Go5200 64M,
monitor=cinema vgasize=1152x768x32
ethernet: Intel 82801DB PRO/100 VE (MOB) (i82557), works
disk controller: Intel 82801DBM (ICH4-M) IDE Controller, works
audio: Intel 82801DB/DBL/DBM (ICH4/ICH4-L/ICH4-M) AC'97 Audio Controller, works
usb: Intel 82801DB/DBL/DBM (ICH4/ICH4-L/ICH4-M) USB UHCI Controller, untested

3.2.6 – Desktops

3.2.6.1 – eMachines

T3302 cpu: AMD Sempron 3300+ 2GHz
chipset: VIA K8M800
graphics: VIA S3 UniChrome, replaced with NVidia GeoForce FX 5700 128MB DVI output, 1920x1080x32
ethernet: 3Com 3C905-TX Fast Etherlink 10/100 PCI TX
audio:
usb: works

3.2.6.2 – Igel

4210 LX Winestra

3.2.6.3 – Soekris

net6501–70

    cpu: Intel Atom E680 1.6Ghz, both pc and pc64 work
    ethernet: 4x Intel 82574L Gigabit Ethernet, works
    usb: works
    serial console: works, use `console=0 b19200` in plan9.ini. 9boot hangs without a serial cable attached; disable uartputc as a workaround
    this machine does not have ACPI

3.2.6.4 – IBM/Lenovo

3.2.6.4.1 – ThinkCentre

M55

8810–D3U

    cpu: Intel Core 2 Duo
    graphics: Intel GMA 3000 internal (untested), replaced with NVidia GeForce 8400GS DVI output, `realemu(8) monitor=vesa vgasize=1680x1050x32`
    ethernet: Broadcom BCM5755 (10/100/1000), works
    audio: Intel HDA, works
    usb: works
    mp: mp + sata, ethernet, usb works with `*acpi=`

M920q

    cpu: Intel 8th Gen Core i5-8500T @ 2.1GHz
    dvd: works
    efi boot: works
    ethernet: Intel I219-LM, works
    graphics: Intel UHD 630, VESA works

    xhci: works

3.3 – Virtual Machines

9front has been tested on several virtual machines. Details below.

Note: As a general rule it is a good idea to manually specify a unique MAC address for each virtual machine instance running on the network, to avoid collisions.

3.3.1 – Qemu

The following generic setup is tested with qemu 1.5.0 and 2.0.50 running on Linux, using *FQA 3.3.3 – virtio* for disk and network. This same generic setup should work for most host operating systems.

3.3.1.1 – Installation

Create a sparse disk image:

```
qemu-img create -f qcow2 9front.qcow2.img 30G
```

Boot the 9front.iso:

```
qemu-system-x86_64 -cpu host -enable-kvm -m 1024 \
-net nic,model=virtio,macaddr=52:54:00:00:EE:03 -net user \
-device virtio-scsi-pci,id=scsi \
-drive if=none,id=vd0,file=9front.qcow2.img \
-device scsi-hd,drive=vd0 \
-drive if=none,id=vd1,file=9front.iso \
-device scsi-cd,drive=vd1,bootindex=0
```

Finally, see: *FQA 4.3 – Performing a simple install*

3.3.1.2 – Post-Installation Booting

```
qemu-system-x86_64 -cpu host -enable-kvm -m 1024 \
-net nic,model=virtio,macaddr=52:54:00:00:EE:03 -net user \
-device virtio-scsi-pci,id=scsi \
-drive if=none,id=vd0,file=9front.qcow2.img \
-device scsi-hd,drive=vd0
```

3.3.1.2.1 – Multiboot

Multiboot can be used to start the 9front kernel directly, skipping the bootloader step:

```
-qemu -kernel 9pc -initrd plan9.ini
```

3.3.1.4 – Networking

User networking is the default and works the same on every platform. More advanced options are particular to specific host operating systems; several are described below.

Note: On many operating systems ICMP is limited to the superuser. One consequence is that a VM running with guest networking cannot ping remote hosts.

3.3.1.4.1 – Linux VDE

Install vde2.

Setup a tap interface:

```
sudo tunctl -u $USER -t tap0
```

Start a virtual switch connected to the tap interface:

```
vde_switch --tap tap0 -daemon
```

Connect the switch to the network of the host. Use DHCP:

```
slirpvde --dhcp --daemon
```

When booting 9front, add the following to the qemu command line arguments:

```
-net vde
```

3.3.1.4.2 – OpenBSD TAP

Tested: OpenBSD/amd64 6.0-STABLE, qemu-2.6.0

Note: Read over this first. Be careful not to clobber any system settings you may already have configured. If you don't understand something, read the relevant man pages until you do. Feel free to substitute arbitrary network values below.

```
# as root
pkg_add bzip2 plan9port qemu ssvnc wget
cp -f /usr/local/plan9/bin/rc /bin/       # for scripts
sysctl net.inet.ip.forwarding=1
echo  'net.inet.ip.forwarding=1' >>/etc/sysctl.conf
echo inet 192.168.54.1 255.255.255.0 NONE >/etc/hostname.vether0
ed /etc/pf.conf
/ext_if
a
int_if="vether0"

match out from $int_if:network to any nat-to ($ext_if:0)
.
w
q
pfctl -f /etc/pf.conf
echo link0 up >/etc/hostname.tap0
echo add vether0 add tap0 up >/etc/hostname.bridge0
sh /etc/netstart
>/etc/dhcpd.conf
ed /etc/dhcpd.conf
i
option domain-name "example.com";
option domain-name-servers 192.168.54.1;

subnet 192.168.54.0 netmask 255.255.255.0 {
        option routers 192.168.54.1;

        range 192.168.54.100 192.168.54.199;
}
.
w
q
rcctl enable dhcpd
rcctl start dhcpd
ed /var/unbound/etc/unbound.conf
/interface
a
        interface: 192.168.54.1
.
/access-control
a
        access-control: 192.168.54.0/24 allow
w
q
rcctl enable unbound
rcctl start unbound
echo 'permit setenv { -ENV PS1=$DOAS PS1 SSH AUTH SOCK } :wheel' \
        >/etc/doas.conf

# as user who is in wheel group
mkdir -p $HOME/9 $HOME/bin
cd $HOME/9
qemu-img -f qcow2 9front.qcow2.img 30G
# adjust url for current iso
wget http://9front.org/iso/9front-5561.df1dc1ff2475.iso.bz2
bunzip2 9front-5561.df1dc1ff2475.iso.bz2
mv 9front-5561.df1dc1ff2475.iso 9front.iso
cd $HOME/bin
```

```
wget http://openbsd.stanleylieber.com/rc/q9
chmod 775 q9
cd
# boot from iso (install)
doas -u root q9 -i
# boot from qcow image (after completing the install)
doas -u root q9
# connect to qemu via vnc
q9 -v
```

3.3.1.4.3 – Windows TAP

This is tested with the qemu for windows distribution. Download and run the installer from openvpn to install the windows TAP driver. Create a new TAP interface with the "Add a new TAP virtual ethernet adapter" from the openvpn start menu. Go to the network manager and rename that new TAP interface to something more sane like: "qemu-tap". Configure ip addresses or bridge that interface with the network manager.

Now you should be able to run qemu on that interface:

```
qemu.exe -net nic -net tap,ifname="tap-qemu" ...
```

3.3.1.4.4 – Linux TAP

Contributed by joe9:

on the host:

```
sudo ip tuntap add dev tap0 mode tap user joe
sudo ip address add 10.0.0.1/24 dev tap0
```

start qemu using (do not need sudo for qemu):

```
SDL_VIDEO_X11_DGAMOUSE=0 qemu-system-x86_64 \
        -cpu host -enable-kvm -m 1024 \
        -netdev tap,id=eth,ifname=tap0,script=no,downscript=no \
        -device e1000,netdev=eth,mac=52:54:00:00:EE:03 \
        -device virtio-scsi-pci,id=scsi -drive \
        if=none,id=vd0,file=9front.qcow2.img \
        -device scsi-hd,drive=vd0 \
        -usb -usbdevice tablet -sdl \
        -ctrl-grab
```

on 9front: add the below line to /lib/ndb/local

```
sys=cirno ether=52540000ee03 ip=10.0.0.2 ipmask=255.255.255.0
        ipgw=10.0.0.1
        dns=10.0.0.1
        dom=cirno.9front
```

run: ip/ipconfig -N

Now, "ping 10.0.0.2" from linux host and "ip/ping 10.0.0.1" from qemu 9front should work.

check the communication between the vm and the linux host using (on the linux host):

```
sudo tcpdump -nS -vv -i tap0
```

Contributed by hiro:

If you want to enable internet access enable NAT forwarding on the linux host (as root).

To do this, first globally enable forwarding:

```
echo 1 > /proc/sys/net/ipv4/ip_forward
```

Enable Masquerading for everything comping from the VM's tap device (eth0 being your host's way to the internet):

```
iptables -t nat -A POSTROUTING -s 10.0.0.0/24 -o eth0 -j MASQUERADE
```

block everything else from being forwarded:

```
iptables -A FORWARD -m state --state RELATED,ESTABLISHED -j ACCEPT
iptables -A FORWARD -s 10.0.0.0/24 -i tap0 -j ACCEPT
iptables -P FORWARD DROP
```

3.3.1.5 – Audio

Run qemu with the flag `-soundhw sb16` and put the following line in `plan9.ini`:

```
audio0=type=sb16 port=0x220 irq=5 dma=5
```

Note: `irq` and `dma` values may vary.

3.3.1.6 – Graphics

Use `monitor-vesa`

Note: Some versions of QEMU running on OSX have exhibited graphical glitches when using a 16-bit color mode (for example: 1024x768x16. Try a 32-bit mode instead (for example: 1024x768x32).

3.3.2 – Virtualbox

Don't use Virtualbox. It tends to break between versions.

Read: `http://www.landley.net/notes-2015.html#25-06-2015`

If you can't be dissuaded, the following sections detail empircal observations re: Virtualbox.

3.3.2.1 – Ethernet The emulated "Intel PRO/1000 MT Server" ethernet controller is known to work.

3.3.2.2 – Audio

Put the following in `plan9.ini`:

```
audio0=type=sb16
```

3.3.2.3 – Graphics Use `monitor=vesa`

3.3.2.4 – Known Working Versions

4.3.14 r95030 on Windows 7

4.3.16 on Mac OS X

4.3.18 r96516 on Linux x86_64 kernel 3.14.22

4.3.18 on Windows 7:

just tried with vbox 4.3.18 on windows7. 9front boots fine in BIOS mode, but the PCnet nic dosnt work. reason is that vbox pIIx pci irq routing is fucked so the ethernet doesnt get interrupts. if i boot with *nopcirouting=1, it works fine. theres a option to select the chipset so i tried ICH9 with IO-APIC enabled. normal mp mode fails because of broken mp tables, but works with *acpi=. also, it works with UEFI mode (which always uses ACPI). the usual intel mt server nic also works (thats what is usually recommended for working arround the broken ethernet).

pci routing issue has been fixed in latest kernel, should be available in iso release after 3960.

4.3.20 r96996 on Mac OS X 10.6.8/10.9 and Ubuntu 14.04/14.10:

```
General -> Basic
Type: Other
Version: Other/Uknown

System -> Motherboard
Chipset: PIIX3
Pointing Device: PS/2 Mouse
Extended Features: [x] Enable I/O APIC

System -> Processor
Extended Features: [x] PAE/NX (not sure this matters)

System -> Acceleration
[x] Enable VT-x/AMD-V
[x] Enable Nested Paging

Display -> Video
Extended Features: [x] Enable 3D Acceleration (not sure this matters)

Storage -> Attributes
Name: IDE
Type: PIIX4
[x] Use Host I/O Cache

Audio ->
[x] Enable Audio
Host Audio Driver: CoreAudio (Can be PulseAudio or otherwise for Linux,
etc. Shouldn't be hard to set this)
Audio Controller: Soundblaster 16

Network -> Adapter 1
Attached to: NAT
-> Advanced
Adapter Type: Intel PRO/1000 MT Server
Promiscuous Mode: Deny (Not sure this matters)
```

Note: Enabling USB 2.0 Controll in 'Ports -> USB' works just fine in 9front, mounting under /shr flawlessly as long as the host has the Virtualbox Extension Pack running.

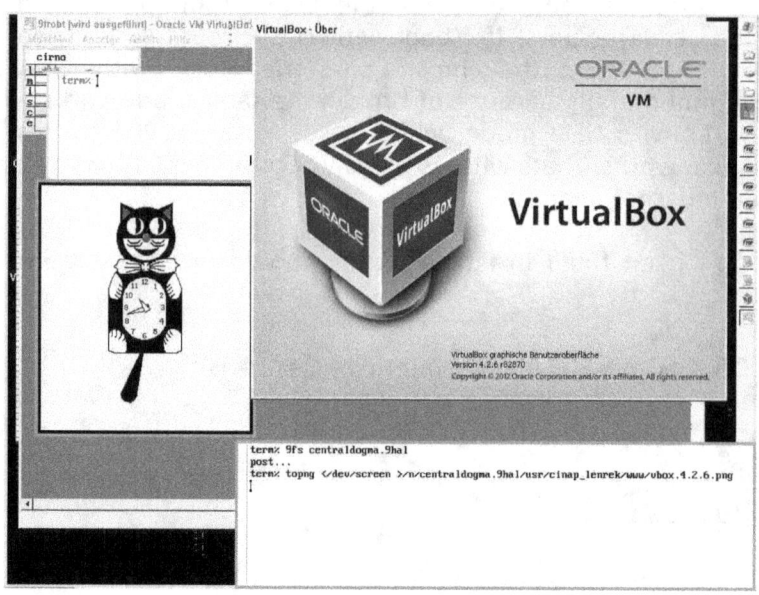

3.3.3 – Virtio

Current versions of qemu/kvm and virtualbox as of 3.1 support faster paravirtualized devices. Presently, 9front provides drivers for virtio hard disk and network.

The virtio-blk disk device should show up as: `/dev/sdF0`

The virtio-scsi disk device should show up as: `/dev/sd00`

FQA 4 – 9front Installation Guide

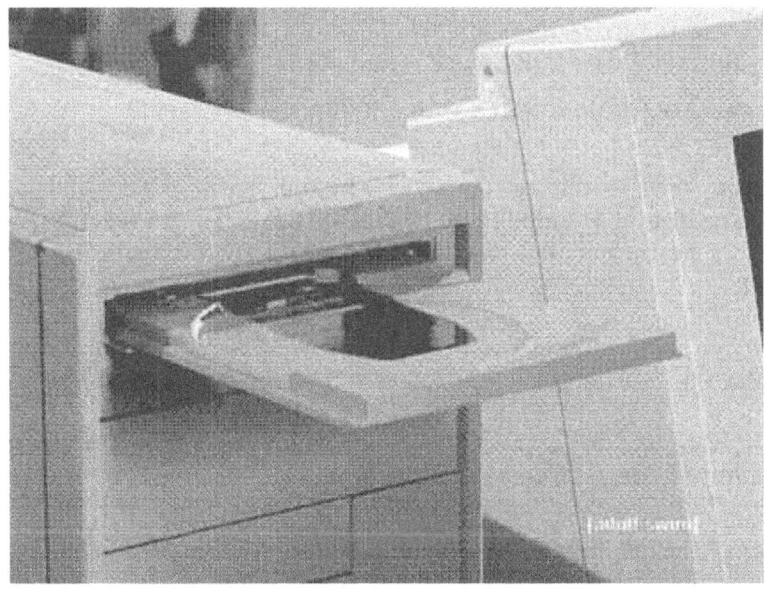

4.1 – Pre–installation Checklist

Before you start your install, you should have some idea what you want to end up with. You will want to know the following items, at least:

Machine name, hereafter referred to as sysname.

Hardware installed and available. Read: *FQA 3.3 – Selecting Hardware.* Check *FQA 3.2 – Known Working Hardware* as well as the various supported hardware pages on the Bell Labs Plan 9 wiki to help determine if your hardware or VM is supported.

Network settings, if not using DHCP: Gather the requisite information for your network (IP, netmask, default gateway, etc.). If you plan to install in a VM, see *FQA 3.3 – Virtual Machines.*

In case of trouble, see: *FQA 9 – Troubleshooting, FQA 2.2.1 – Mailing List Archives*

4.2 – Creating bootable 9front install media

4.2.1 – ISO image

Obtain the 9front.iso.

Read: *1.11.1 – Mirrors*

4.2.2 – USB drive

Booting from USB disk is handled the same way as booting from internal hard drive. There are two ways to create a bootable 9front USB:

1.) Write the ISO image directly to the USB device. Example:

```
cat 9front.iso >/dev/sdUxxxxx/data
```

2.) Alternately, the boot process is able to use an ISO image stored on a FAT file system as its root file system, so all that is needed is to install the 9boot(8) bootloader, a kernel and the 9front.iso on the USB disk. The following sections describe this process on Plan 9 and Linux.

4.2.2.1 – Creating on Plan 9

The path to your USB device will look something like this: /dev/sdUxxxxx where xxxxx is the unique name of your usb device.

Build and install the mbr and boot loader:

```
cd /sys/src/boot/pc
mk 9bootfat mbr pbs
disk/mbr -m mbr /dev/sdUxxxxx/data
```

If it doesn't already exist, create and format a FAT partition. Don't forget to set the FAT partition active in the fdisk menu:

```
disk/fdisk -b /dev/sdUxxxxx/data
disk/format -b pbs -d -r 2 /dev/sdUxxxxx/dos
```

Mount the USB device:

```
dossrv -f /dev/sdUxxxxx/dos sdos
mount -c /srv/sdos /n/dos
```

Create a suitable /n/dos/plan9.ini:

```
bootfile=9pc
mouseport=ask
monitor=ask
vgasize=ask
```

Note: By convention, Plan 9 usually expects text files to end with a newline. If the last line of plan9.ini is not a newline, it could fail to be parsed correctly at boot time.

Copy files to the USB device:

```
cp /386/9bootfat /n/dos
chmod +al /n/dos/9bootfat # defrag magic
cp /386/9pc /n/dos
cp /path/to/9front.iso /n/dos
```

Optional for EFI systems:

```
cd /sys/src/boot/efi; mk install
mkdir -p /n/dos/efi/boot
cp /386/boot*.efi /n/dos/efi/boot
```

Unmount the USB device:

```
unmount /n/dos
rm -f /srv/sdos
```

Boot the device.

Read: prep(8)

4.2.2.2 – Creating on Linux

Note: There are numerous methods for creating bootable USB devices on Linux. This is one.

Obtain mbr, pbs, 9bootfat and 9pc binaries. Either copy them from the distributed ISO image (the files are located under /386/) or build up to date binaries on a 9front system. Read: *FQA 5.2.2 – Building from source*

On the Linux system, create a $dir with that contains the following files:

```
9front.iso
9pc
plan9.ini (as described above)
9bootfat
mbr
pbs
```

Optional for EFI systems, create the directory boot in $dir and copy the files bootia32.efi and bootx64.efi into it.

Use the makebootfat tool to create bootable device (ie. /dev/sdc):

```
$ makebootfat -m $dir/mbr -b $dir/pbs -o /dev/sdc $dir
```

Boot the device.

4.2.2.3 – Bootargs

At the bootargs prompt you'll need to enter the path to the ISO on the USB device. It will look something like this:

```
bootargs=local!/shr/sdUxxxxx/9front.iso
```

If a USB device is not listed, escape to a shell with !rc, and ls /shr to find it.

Read: 9.5.1 – Devices not recognized or not working

4.3 – Performing a simple install

There is nothing magical about installing Plan 9. It is simply a matter of populating a Plan 9 file system (`cwfs` or `hjfs`) and arranging a bootstrap to eventually load a Plan 9 kernel that can then use that file system as its root.

In most cases, the file server is the only machine that needs to have a disk. Once the initial file server is running, setting up an auth server, and enabling `bootp` and `tftp` for PXE booting, will allow Plan 9 terminals and cpu servers to load kernels from the file server and share its file system over the network.

Note: This guide describes the default installation of a terminal with disk, which is an amalgamation of a normal Plan 9 network, but is sufficient for exploring the basics of using Plan 9. Configuration of additional services (such as a file server with networking listeners, a cpu server, etc.) is outlined in *FQA 7 – System Management*.

To install 9front, boot the `9front.iso` image and follow the steps below.

4.3.1 – boot

Successfully booting the system will result in basic information about the state of the system being printed on screen:

```
Plan 9
126 holes free
00018000 0009f000 552960
00485000 0cf2c000 212496384
213049344 bytes free
cpu0: 3395MHz GenuineIntel P6
ELCR: 0E20
#l0: AMD79C970: 10Mbps port 0x2000 irq 10: 000c291d0baf
mylex ctlr @ port 0x10c0: 32-bit wide SCSI host adapter
512M memory: 207M kernel data, 304M user, 929M swap
nusb/usbd: /dev/usb: no hubs
```


4.3.2 – bootargs

A list of attached storage devices is printed, followed by a prompt asking for a Plan 9 partition to boot from:

```
/dev/sdC0: VMware Virtual IDE Hard Drive
/dev/sdC0/data
/dev/sdD0: VMware Virtual IDE CDROM Drive
/dev/sdD0/data 9660
bootargs is (tcp, il, local!device) [local!/dev/sdD0/data]
```

In most cases, the suggested default will correspond to the device used to boot the ISO image.

4.3.3 – user

Next, a prompt asks for a username:

```
user[glenda]:
```

Glenda is the default `hostowner` name. Don't change this until you know what you are doing. Hit `enter` to accept the default.

Note: The `hostowner` differs from the concept of `root` on a UNIX system, where a single user `root` may take control of all processes *and* files on the system. By contrast, even the `hostowner` of a Plan 9 file server cannot violate file permissions on the file system, except when permissions checking is disabled on the console or when entering special commands at the console of the file server. The `hostowner` controls only the *processes* running on the local machine (in the case of the filserver, the file server process itself is obviously owned by the system's `hostowner`). This fundamental separation between control of processes and file permissions is exploited throughout the system, but can be confusing for users coming from a UNIX background.

4.3.4 – vgasize, monitor, mouseport

The next set of prompts deal with graphics display and the mouse:

```
vgasize is (text, 640x480x8, 1024x768x16, ...) [1024x768x16]
monitor is (vesa, xga, lcd, ...) [vesa]
mouseport is (ps2, ps2intellimouse, 0, 1, 2) [ps2]
```

The boot process prompts for the environment variables $vgasize, $monitor and $mouseport, and the installer will later write those values to the system's `plan9.ini`, from which they are loaded on subsequent system bootup.

Setting $monitor to anything besides `vesa` will bypass the emulated VESA BIOS and attempt to use a native VGA driver for the video card in question. Read: `/lib/vgadb` for a list of monitors and video cards that are already known by the system; and the man pages `vga(3)`, `vga(8)` and `vgadb(6)` for more information about how graphical displays are configured.

The default $mouseport of `ps2` is sufficient in most cases. Set it to `ps2intellimouse` on laptops or for mice that have a scrollwheel.

Note: Some laptops require the trackpad to be disabled in the BIOS in order for mouse button 2 (the center button) to function in Plan 9. In a pinch, mouse button 2 may be simulated by holding down the `shift` key while clicking mouse button 3 (the right button).

After the install, changes intended to persist across reboots should be added to `plan9.ini`.

Examples:

Values as they appear in `plan9.ini`:

```
monitor=vesa
vgasize=1024x768x16
mouseport=ps2intellimouse
```

Read: mouse(8), vga(3), vgadb(6), plan9.ini(8), realemu(8), vga(8), *FQA 7.2.2 – How do I modify plan9.ini?*

After the mouseport prompt is answered, the boot process will attempt to start the Plan 9 graphical environment, rio(1), opening a stats(8) window and a rio window on top of a gray desktop background.

4.3.4.1 – Changing screen resolution

At this point it may be desireable to change the screen resolution. To change video mode from the command line:

vesa:

Note: Only valid modes listed in the VESA BIOS may be used.

```
# obtain a list of vesa bios modes
@{rfork n; aux/realemu; aux/vga -p}
# configure one of the valid modes
@{rfork n; aux/realemu; aux/vga -m vesa -l 1024x768x16}
```

vga:

```
aux/vga -m dellst2210 -l 1920x1080x32
```

4.3.5 – inst/start

Installation is performed by the rc scripts in `/rc/bin/inst`. To begin the installation, type `inst/start` in the terminal window. Follow the prompts to complete the installation, selecting the defaults where appropriate.

Note: Any task may be repeated by manually entering its name at the next `Task to do` prompt.

```
term% inst/start
Tue Jul 17 12:38:50 CET 2012 Installation process started
```

The following `Task to do` steps are handled one at a time:

4.3.6 – configfs

```
You can install the following types of systems:

    cwfs64x      the cached-worm file server
    hjfs         the new 9front file server (experimental!)

File system (cwfs64x, hjfs)[cwfs64x]:
```

Note: The `cwfs64x` file server uses 16KB blocks, with its cache and permanent storage locate on separate partitions. The `hjfs` file server uses 4KB blocks, with its cache and permanent storage located on the same partition. If you are installing to a disk of less than 12GB, you should choose `hjfs`.

In this example we will press `enter` to accept `cwfs64x` as the default.

4.3.6.1 – cwfs no–dump configuration A cheap VPS or an SD card lack the storage capacity for running a usable default `cwfs(4)` setup with a big WORM partition and daily dumps. The go-to solution is the `hjfs(4)` file system, which doesn't use a dedicated WORM partition and doesn't do daily dumps by default. However, it has several performance problems and is not as well tested.

The 'cwfs' file system can be configured in lots of ways beyond the default cache-worm + other configuration supported by the 9front installer.

The desired configuration we're going to cover is a single 'main' file server tree backed by a simple disk file system – the same type used by the 'other' tree in the default setup.

To do this we're going to partition the disk appropriately and override the 'mountcwfs' stage of the 9front installer with a replacement script http://a-b.xyz/23/666a that will configure 'cwfs' appropriately. The rest of the installation and most of the subsequent system operation remain unaffected.

Start by booting from the installation media. Configure networking with 'ip/ipconfig(8)' and fetch the replacement 'mountcwfs' script, or put the script on a flash drive:

```
% webfs
% ramfs
% hget http://a-b.xyz/23/666a >/tmp/mountcwfs
% chmod +x /tmp/mountcwfs
```

Override the 'mountcwfs' stage using 'bind(1)':

```
bind /tmp/mountcwfs /bin/inst/mountcwfs
```

Run 'inst/start' and complete the stages up to 'preppart' as you would normally. At 'preppart', delete the default partitions and create one named 'fsmain' with a desired size:

```
d other
d fscache
d fsworm
a fsmain 123456 .+100%
w
q
```

Make sure to "ream" the new partition at the next step.

Complete the rest of the installation, reboot. That is all.

4.3.7 – partdisk

```
The following disk devices were found.

sdC0 - VMware Virtual IDE Hard Drive
    empty                   0 3916          (3916 cylinders, 29.99 GB)

sdD0 - VMware Virtual IDE CDROM Drive

Disk to partition (sdC0, sdD0)[no default]:
```

Enter the media you wish to install to.

```
Disk to partition (sdC0, sdD0)[no default]: sdC0
The disk you selected HAS NO master boot record on its first sector.
(Perhaps it is a completely blank disk.)
Shall we create a blank EFI partition table (GPT)
or install traditional DOS partition table (MBR)?
```

Assuming a blank disk image, install a fresh mbr:

```
Install mbr or gpt (mbr, gpt)[no default]: mbr

This is disk/fdisk; use it to create a Plan 9 partition.
If there is enough room, a Plan 9 partition will be
suggested; you can probably just type 'w' and then 'q'.

cylinder = 8225280 bytes
>>>
```

For this example we will use the entire disk. Accept the defaults.

```
>>> w
>>> q
```

4.3.8 – prepdisk

```
The following Plan 9 disk partitions were found.

/dev/sdC0/plan9
  empty                   0 62910477    (62910477 sectors, 29.99 GB)

Plan 9 partition to subdivide (/dev/sdC0/plan9)[/dev/sdC0/plan9]:
```

Use the Plan 9 partition created in the previous step. Hit 'enter' to select the default.

```
This is disk/prep; use it to subdivide the Plan 9 partition.
If it is not yet subdivided, a sensible layout will be suggested;
you can probably just type 'w' and then 'q'.

no plan9 partition table found
9fat 204800
nvram 1
other 8957953
fscache 8957953
fsworm 44789770
>>>
```

Again, accept the defaults.

```
>>> w
>>> q
```

4.3.9 – mountfs

```
The please choose your cwfs64x partitions
```

Hit enter to select each partition at the prompt.

```
--rw-r----- S 0 glenda glenda 4586471936 Jul  4 13:28 /dev/sdC0/fscache

Cwfs cache partition (/dev/sdC0/fscache)[/dev/sdC0/fscache]:
--rw-r----- S 0 glenda glenda 22932362240 Jul  4 13:28 /dev/sdC0/fsworm

Cwfs worm partition (/dev/sdC0/fsworm)[/dev/sdC0/fsworm]:
--rw-r----- S 0 glenda glenda 4586471936 Jul  4 13:28 /dev/sdC0/other

Cwfs other partition (/dev/sdC0/other)[/dev/sdC0/other]:
```

Since this is a fresh install, we choose yes to ream (format) the file system:

```
Ream the file system? (yes, no)[no]: yes
Starting cwfs64x file server for /dev/sdC0/fscache
Reaming file system
bad nvram key
bad authentication id
bad authentication domain
nvrcheck: can't read nvram
config: config: config: auth is now disabled
config: config: config: config: config: config: current fs is "main"
cmd_users: cannot access /adm/users
63-bit cwfs as of Wed Jul  4 00:59:30 2012
        last boot Tue Jul 17 13:34:57 2012
Configuering cwfs64x file server for /dev/sdC0/fscache
Mounting cwfs64x file server for /dev/sdC0/fscache
% mount -c /srv/cwfs /n/newfs
Mounting cwfs64x file server for /dev/sdC0/other
% mount -c /srv/cwfs /n/other other
```

4.3.10 – configdist

```
Are you going to download the distribution
from the internet or do you have it on local media?

Distribution is from (local, net)[local]:
```

We are installing from local media, so, local. Hit 'enter' to accept the default.

Note: The net option attempts to download the ISO from the Internet and install it directly to disk. Since the installer is most likely already running from an ISO image, this option may prove to be of limited utility. The option is somewhat experimental, and may work. Attempt it at your own risk.

4.3.11 – confignet

```
You can connect to the internet via
a local ethernet or a dial-up PPP connection.

Interface to use (ether, ppp)[ether]:

Please choose a method for configuring your ethernet connection.

        manual - specify IP address, network mask, gateway IP address
        dhcp - use DHCP to automatically configure

Configuration method (manual, dhcp)[dhcp]:
```

4.3.11.1 – dhcp

Hit enter to move on to the next task.

4.3.11.2 – manual

If you chose manual, enter values that are appropriate for your network.

```
Configuration method (manual, dhcp)[dhcp]: manual
ip address [no default]: 10.0.2.15
network mask [no default]: 255.255.255.0
gateway address [no default]: 10.0.2.2
```

4.3.12 – mountdist

```
Please wait... Scanning storage devices...
        /dev/sdC0/9fat
        /dev/sdC0/data
        /dev/sdC0/fscache
        /dev/sdC0/fsworm
        /dev/sdC0/other
        /dev/sdD0/data

The following storage media were detected.
Choose the one containing the distribution.

        /dev/sdD0/data (iso9660 cdrom)

Distribution disk (/dev/sdD0/data, /dev/sdC0/fscache, /)[/]:
```

The CD-ROM is already mounted at /, so we hit enter to choose the default.

```
% mount /srv/boot /n/distmedia

Which directory contains the distribution?
Any of the following will suffice (in order of preference):
        - the root directory of the cd image
        - the directory containing 9front.iso
        - the directory containing 9front.iso.bz2

Location of archives [/]:
```

And again, the root directory of the CD-ROM is already mounted at /, so hit enter to choose the default.

```
% mount /srv/boot /n/distmedia

Which directory contains the distribution?
Any of the following will suffice (in order of preference):
        - the root directory of the cd image
        - the directory containing 9front.iso
        - the directory containing 9front.iso.bz2

Location of archives [/]:
```

Hit enter.

4.3.13 – copydist Hit `enter` at the `copydist` prompt to begin the process of copying the distribution files from the install media to the hard disk.

```
processing /sys/lib/sysconfig/proto/allproto
```

ACHTUNG! Currently, there is no progress meter. For systems without DMA, the `copydist` task may exceed one hour in duration. Disk activity may be verified by inspecting the `stats(8)` window.

Eventually, you should see the following:

```
file system made
```

This indicates that the system files have completed copying to the install target.

4.3.14 – sysname

```
Setup network configuration

sysname [cirno]:
```

Use a system name of your choice, or just hit enter to select the default.

4.3.15 – tzsetup

```
Setup Time Zone

Time Zone (Argentina, Australia_ACT, Australia_Broken-Hill,
Australia_LHI, Australia_NSW, Australia_North, Australia_Queensland,
Australia_South, Australia_Sturt, Australia_Tasmania,
Australia_Victoria, Australia_West, Australia_Yancowinna, Brazil_Acre,
Brazil_DeNoronha, Brazil_East, Brazil_West, CET, Canada_Atlantic,
Canada_Central, Canada_East Saskatchewan, Canada_Eastern,
Canada_Mountain, Canada_Newfoundland, Canada_Pacific, Canada_Yukon,
Chile_Continental, Chile_EasterIsland, Cuba, EET, Egypt, GB-Eire, GMT,
HST, Hongkong, Iceland, Iran, Israel, Jamaica, Japan, Libya,
Mexico_BajaNorte, Mexico_BajaSur, Mexico_General, NZ, NZ_CHAT, Navajo,
PRC, Poland, ROC, ROK, Singapore, Turkey, US_Alaska, US_Arizona,
US_Central, US_East-Indiana, US_Eastern, US_Hawaii, US_Michigan,
US_Mountain, US_Pacific, US_Yukon, W-SU, WET)[US_Eastern]:
```

Daylight saving time (DST) is handled automatically. Type your chosen time zone and hit enter.

4.3.16 – bootsetup

```
Setup Plan 9 FAT boot partition (9fat)

Plan 9 FAT partition (/dev/sdC0/9fat)[/dev/sdC0/9fat]:
```

Hit enter to accept the default. Any environment variables entered at the > prompt during boot, as well as settings configured during install will now be written to /n/9fat/plan9.ini and the kernel will be copied to the 9fat partition.

```
dossrv: serving #s/dos
Initializing Plan 9 FAT partition.
% disk/format -r 2 -d -b /386/pbs /dev/sdC0/9fat
Initializing FAT file system
type hard, 12 tracks, 255 heads, 63 sectors/track, 512 bytes/sec
used 4096 bytes
% mount -c /srv/dos /n/9fat /dev/sdC0/9fat
% rm -f /n/9fat/9bootfat /n/9fat/plan9.ini /n/9fat/9pc
% cp /n/newfs/386/9bootfat /n/9fat/9bootfat
% chmod +al /n/9fat/9bootfat
% cp /tmp/plan9.ini /n/9fat/plan9.ini
% cp /n/newfs/386/9pc /n/9fat/9pc

If you use the Windows NT/2000/XP master boot record
or a master boot record from a Unix clone (e.g., LILO or
FreeBSD bootmgr), it is probably safe to continue using
that boot record rather than install the Plan 9 boot record.
```

Since we are not installing on a disk with a pre-existing Windows installation, we choose to install the Plan 9 master boot record and mark the partition active:

```
Install the Plan 9 master boot record (y, n)[no default]: y
Mark the Plan 9 partition active (y, n)[no default]: y

The Plan 9 partition is now marked as active.
```

4.3.17 – finish

The final task is to remove (or disable) the CD-ROM and finish by hitting enter to reboot the machine.

Congratulations, you've just installed a 9front system!

Now your cat goes to sleep on the keyboard.

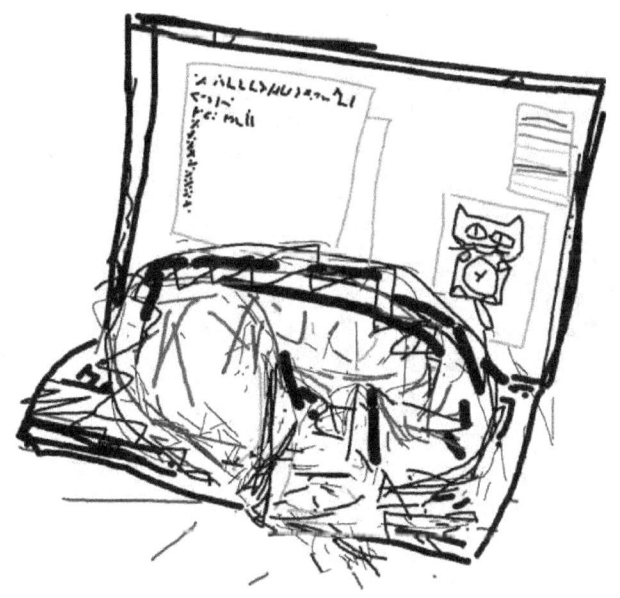

4.4 – Encrypted Partitions

9front supports booting from encrypted `fsworm`, `fscache` and `other` partitions. The following assumes a hard drive `/dev/sdC0`:

- Begin the installation process as normal by booting `9front.iso`.

- During `partdisk` and `prepdisk`, create the `fsworm`, `fscache` and `other` partitions as normal.

- At the `mountfs` prompt, enter `!rc` to drop to a shell prompt.

- Format and activate the encrypted partitions (generates new encryption key):

```
disk/cryptsetup -f /dev/sdC0/fsworm /dev/sdC0/fscache /dev/sdC0/other
disk/cryptsetup -i /dev/sdC0/fsworm /dev/sdC0/fscache /dev/sdC0/other
```

- Type `exit` to resume the installation.

- During `mountfs`, select the partitions under `/dev/fs` instead of the ones under `/dev/sdC0`.

- During the rest of the installation, select the defaults, where appropriate.

- During post-installation boot, at the `bootargs` prompt, type `!rc` to drop to a shell prompt.

- Activate the encrypted partitions (prompts for password):

```
disk/cryptsetup -i /dev/sdC0/fsworm /dev/sdC0/fscache /dev/sdC0/other
```

- Type `exit` to resume booting.

- At the `bootargs` prompt, enter `local!/dev/fs/fscache` to continue booting from the encrypted partition.

Note: Encrypted partitians are largely untested. Data integrity is not guaranteed. Use at your own risk.

Encrypted partitions have not been tested with `hjfs`.

Read: `cryptsetup(8)`

FQA 5 – Building the System from Source

5.1 – Why should I build my system from source?

Some reasons why you might actually wish or need to build from source:
- Updates have been committed since you performed the installation.

- Test or develop new features.

5.2 – Building 9front from source

5.2.1 – Update sources

9front uses git(1) to synchronize the system with the 9front repository:

```
cd /
bind -ac /dist/plan9front /
git/pull -u gits://git.9front.org/plan9front/plan9front
```

which is consolidated in the command:

```
sysupdate
```

After the tree is updated, recompile/build the updated programs as needed.

5.2.1.1 – hgrc

5.2.1.2 – git

During installation, the 9front git repository is copied to /dist/plan9front/.git, is chmod 775, and is owned by user glenda and group sys. To update the repository when logged in as a user other than glenda, add that user to group sys.

5.2.2 – Building from source

Note: A minimum of 512MB RAM is needed to link some programs. If less than 512MB is available, be sure to turn on swap before building (Read: swap(8)).

```
# create any missing directories needed for the build
cd /
. /sys/lib/rootstub

# build everything
cd /sys/src
mk install
mk clean

# build manpage indices
cd /sys/man
mk

# build the papers and html (optional)
cd /sys/doc
mk
mk html
```

Note: Before cross compiling a kernel, the compiler, assembler, linker, and paqfs(4) for the target architecture need to be built and installed (Read *FQA 5.2.2.1 – Cross compiling).*

Build the kernel for 386:

```
cd /sys/src/9/pc
mk install
```

Build the kernel for amd64:

```
cd /sys/src/9/pc64
mk install
```

Build the kernel for arm / Raspberry Pi:

```
cd /sys/src/9/bcm
mk 'CONF=pi' install
mk 'CONF=pi2' install
```

Build the kernel for arm64 / Raspberry Pi 3:

```
cd /sys/src/9/bcm64
mk install
```

Read: *FQA 7.2.5 – How do I install a new kernel?*

5.2.2.1 – Cross compiling

To cross compile, simply set the `objtype` environment variable prior to running the build. For example, to build all the amd64 binaries on a 386 system:

```
# create any missing directories needed for the build
cd /
. /sys/lib/rootstub
cd /sys/src
objtype=amd64 mk install
```

5.3 – Building an ISO

The 9front ISO is a livecd that also serves as install media.

Note: Currently, only the 386 and amd64 architectures have downloadable ISOs (rpi has a bootable image). Read: *FQA 8.9 – Bootstrapping architectures not included on the ISO* for more information on booting other architectures.

```
# put your root file system into /n/src9
bind /root /n/src9

# put your hg repository there
bind -ac /dist/plan9front /n/src9

# build the iso
cd /sys/lib/dist
mk /tmp/9front.$objtype.iso
```

5.4 – Common Problems when Compiling and Building

Most of the time problems in the build process are caused by not following the above directions carefully.

People who complained about this section of the FQA have so far not submitted anything better.

Good luck.

5.4.1 – Updating compilers

Changes to the compilers may necessitate updating the compiler before rebuilding the rest of the system:

```
cd /sys/src/cmd/cc; mk install
# choose the appropriate compiler for your architecture
cd /sys/src/cmd/6c; mk install
```

FQA 6 – Networking

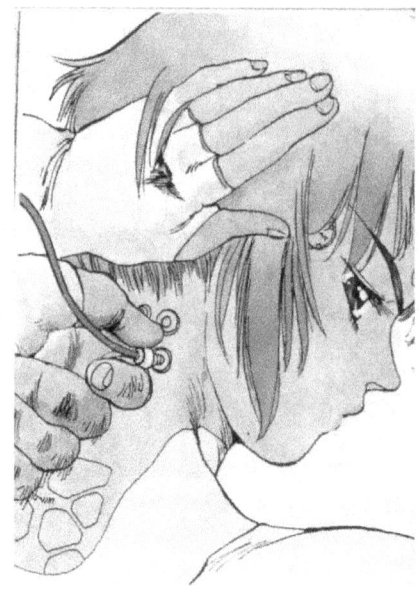

6.1 – Before we go any further

Plan 9's approach to networking is unusual: most operations comprise reading and writing ("composing") byte streams ("files"). For the bulk of this document, it helps if you have read and at least partially understood *FQA 0.1 – What is Plan 9?*

Next, read: *The Organization of Networks in Plan 9*

If you are working with applications such as web servers, FTP servers, and mail servers, you may benefit greatly by reading the RFCs.

Note: A script for downloading all the RFCs is located in `/lib/rfc/grabrfc`. It copies the files into `/lib/rfc/`, and it may take hours for the script to run to completion.

6.2 – Network configuration

Basic networking is initially configured by the installation process. However, more complex settings or services may be desired. In Plan 9, network configuration is organized in `ndb`, the network database.

From `ndb(6)`:

> The network database consists of files describing machines known to the local installation and machines known publicly. The files comprise multi-line tuples made up of attribute/value pairs of the form attr=value or sometimes just attr. Each line starting without white space starts a new tuple. Lines starting with # are comments.

> The file /lib/ndb/local is the root of the database. Other files are included in

the database if a tuple with an attribute-value pair of attribute database and no value exists in /lib/ndb/local. Within the database tuple, each pair with attribute file identifies a file to be included in the database. The files are searched in the order they appear. For example:

```
database=
    file=/lib/ndb/common
    file=/lib/ndb/local
    file=/lib/ndb/global
```

declares the database to be composed of the three files /lib/ndb/common, /lib/ndb/local, and /lib/ndb/global. By default, /lib/ndb/local is searched before the others. How- ever, /lib/ndb/local may be included in the database to redefine its ordering.

Within tuples, pairs on the same line bind tighter than pairs on different lines.

As mentioned, the installer adds basic information about the machine to the file /lib/ndb/local, based on the questions asked during the installation. This file may be edited to modify or expand the definition of the local network.

6.2.1 – Host name

Each machine on the network receives a corresponding section in ndb. The host name (hereafter referred to as sysname) is assigned by setting the sys= tuple:

```
sys=x301
```

The resulting sysname is used by the /rc/bin/termrc and /rc/bin/cpurc startup scripts, which in turn call upon any additional configuration that may exist in /cfg/$sysname/. (Look at the scripts to see how they deal with /cfg.)

6.2.2 – Identifying and setting up your network interfaces

Network interfaces are recognized by their MAC addresses, which are identified to ndb using the ether= tuple:

```
sys=x301 ether=00226811f7dd
```

Additional tuples in the same grouping will be used to configure the interface in question.

6.2.2.1 – WiFi

The following sections provide information pertaining to specific chipsets.

Read: plan9.ini(8), *FQA Section 3.2 – Known Working Hardware*

6.2.2.1.1 – Interfaces

6.2.2.1.1.1 – wavelan

Lucent Wavelan (Orinoco) IEEE 802.11b and compatible PCMCIA cards. Compatible cards include the Dell TrueMobile 1150 and the Linksys Instant Wireless Network PC Card. Port and IRQ defaults are 0x180 and 3 respectively.

These cards take a number of unique options to aid in identifying the card correctly on the 802.11b network. The network may be ad hoc or managed (i.e. use an access point): `mode=[adhoc, managed]` and defaults to managed. The 802.11b network to attach to (managed mode) or identify as (ad hoc mode), is specified by `essid=string` and defaults to a null string. The card station name is given by `station=string` and defaults to Plan 9 STA. The channel to use is given by `channel=number` where number lies in the range 1 to 16 inclusive; the channel is normally negotiated automatically.

If the card is capable of encryption, the following options may be used: `crypt=[off, on]` and defaults to on. `keyN=string` sets the encryption key N (where N is in the range 1 to 4 inclusive) to string; this will also set the transmit key to N (see below). There are two formats for string which depend on the length of the string. If it is exactly 5 or 13 characters long it is assumed to be an alphanumeric key; if it is exactly 10 or 26 characters long the key is assumed to be in hex format (without a leading 0x). The lengths are checked, as is the format of a hex key. `txkey=number` sets the transmit key to use to be number in the range 1 to 4 inclusive. If it is desired to exclude or include unencrypted packets `clear=[off, on]` configures reception and defaults to inclusion.

The defaults are intended to match the common case of a managed network with encryption and a typical entry would only require, for example `essid=left-armpit key1=afish key2=calledraawaru` if the port and IRQ defaults are used. These options may be set after boot by writing to the device's ctl file using a space as the separator between option and value, e.g. `echo 'key2 1d8f65c9a52d83c8e4b43f94af' >/net/ether0/0/ctl` Card-specific power management may be enabled/disabled by `pm=[on, off]`

6.2.2.1.1.2 – wavelanpci

PCI Ethernet adapters that use the same Wavelan programming interface. Currently the only tested cards are those based on the Intersil Prism 2.5 chipset.

6.2.2.1.1.3 – iwl

Intel Wireless WiFi Link mini PCI-Express adapters require firmware from http://firmware.openbsd.org/firmware/iwn-firmware*.tgz to be present on attach in `/lib/firmware` or `/boot`. To select the access point, the `essid=` and `bssid=` parameters can be specified at boot or set during runtime like:

```
echo essid left-armpit >/net/ether1/clone
```

If both `essid=` and `bssid=` are specified, both must match. Scan results appear in the `ifstats` file and can be read out like:

```
cat /net/ether1/ifstats
```

Ad-hoc mode or WEP encryption is currently not supported. To enable WPA/WPA2 encryption, see wpa(8) for details.

6.2.2.1.1.4 – rt2860

Ralink Technology PCI/PCI-Express wireless adapters require firmware from http://firmware.openbsd.org/firmware/ral-firmware*.tgz to be present on attach in /lib/firmware or /boot. See the iwl section above for configuration details.

6.2.2.1.1.5 – wpi

Intel PRO Wireless 3945abg PCI/PCI-Express wireless adapters require firmware from http://firmware.openbsd.org/firmware/*/wpi-firmware*.tgz to be present on attach in /lib/firmware or /boot. See the iwl section above for configuration details.

6.2.2.1.2 – WPA

WPA1/TKIP and WPA2/CCMP are supported with the use of the wpa(8) command.

Read: wpa(8)

6.2.2.1.3 – WiFi Roaming

A script can be used to dynamically re-associate with available wifi access points:

http://plan9.stanleylieber.com/rc/wifiroam

Example usage:

```
@{wifiroam attwifi | aux/statusmsg -k wifiroam} &
```

6.2.2.1.4 – WiFi Debug

For cards that use the wifi layer, debug prints (**note:** will appear on the console) may be enabled with:

```
echo debug >'#l0/ether0/clone'
# change this to suit if wifi interface is not #l0
```

or by adding debug=1 to the interface definition in plan9.ini.

Read: plan9.ini(8)

6.2.3 – IP address

The `ip=` tuple is used to associate an IP address with the machine:

```
sys=x301 ether=00226811f7dd ip=192.168.0.31
```

If no `ip=` tuple is present, the boot scripts will attempt to bring up the interface using DHCP (see below).

6.2.4 – Default gateway

The default gateway is configured using the `ipgw=` tuple, usually under an `ipnet=` section that defines default settings for an entire subnet:

```
ipnet=9front ip=192.168.0.0 ipmask=255.255.255.0 ipgw=192.168.0.1
```

but it may also be specified on a per-machine basis:

```
sys=x301 ether=00226811f7dd ip=192.168.0.31 ipgw=192.168.0.1
```

Note: Tuples included in the definition of a machine supercede those defined for the network to which the machine belongs.

6.2.5 – DNS Resolution

DNS resolvers may be specified using the `dns=` tuple, and may be configured for an entire network:

```
ipnet=9front ip=192.168.0.0 ipmask=255.255.255.0 ipgw=192.168.0.1
        dns=192.168.0.1
```

or on a per-machine basis:

```
sys=x301 ether=00226811f7dd ip=192.168.0.31 dns=192.168.0.1
```

These changes will take effect after a reboot. To configure a DNS resolver on the fly, it is possible to manually edit `/net/ndb`:

```
ip=192.168.0.31 ipmask=255.255.255.0 ipgw=192.168.0.1
        sys=x301
        dom=x301.9front
        dns=192.168.0.1
        # add or modify dns= lines to associate the DNS
        # server 192.168.0.1 with the running system
```

Note: `/net/ndb` is a synthetic file that represents the current operating state. It does not persist across reboots, and is only pre-populated when system networking was configured via DHCP. Changes to a blank `/net/ndb` file will match on the `ip=` tuple.

Read: `ip(3)`

Finally, to turn on debug in `dns`:

```
echo -n debug >/net/dns
```

6.2.5.1 – Caching DNS server

To run a caching DNS server, modify `/cfg/$sysname/termrc` or `/cfg/$sysname/cpurc` (whichever is appropriate) to include the following:

```
ndb/dns -rs
```

The caching DNS server will be started at boot time.

Next, modify `/lib/ndb/local` such that the desired machines will use the IP address of the new caching DNS server as their DNS server, either by changing the `dns=` tuple under the `ipnet` of the corresponding network or by adding a `dns=` tuple to the line of each desired machine.

Read: `ndb(6)` and `ndb(8)`

6.2.5.2 – DNS authoritative name server

An authoritative domain name record, with associated reverse-lookup and sub-domains, looks like this:

```
dom=bell labs.co soa=
        refresh=10800 ttl=10800
        # serial is automatically maintained if omitted
        serial=2012110732
        ns=ns5.he.net
        ns=ns4.he.net
        ns=ns3.he.net
        ns=ns2.he.net
        ns=nm.iawtp.com
        ns=pp.iawtp.com
        ns=mars2.iawtp.com
        dnsslave=slave.dns.he.net
        mb=sl@stanleylieber.com
        mx=pp.inri.net pref=5
        mx=nm.inri.net pref=10
        mx=mars2.inri.net pref=15
        txtrr="v=spf1 mx -all"

dom=125.191.107.in-addr.arpa soa=
        refresh=3600 ttl=3600
        ns=nm.iawtp.com

dom=bell-labs.co ip=107.191.125.208

dom=www.bell-labs.co cname=bell-labs.co
```

An FQDN may be assigned to an existing machine by adding the `dom=` tuple to its definition:

```
sys=x301 dom=x301.bell-labs.co ether=00226811f7dd ip=192.168.0.31
```

Note: The dnsslave entries specify slave DNS servers that should be notified when the domain changes. The notification service also requires the -n flag:

```
ndb/dns -nrs
```

Read: ndb(8)

6.2.5.2.1 – Troubleshooting DNS authoritative name server

An online tool that evaluates the DNS configuration of a given domain name is available
at: https://intodns.com

6.2.6 – Network-wide configuration

Settings for an entire network subnet may be defined under an ipnet= tuple:

```
ipnet=9front ip=192.168.0.0 ipmask=255.255.255.0
        ipgw=192.168.0.1
        auth=192.168.0.2
        authdom=9front
        fs=192.168.0.3
        cpu=192.168.0.4
        dns=192.168.0.1
        dnsdomain=9front
        smtp=192.168.0.4

# ethernet/wifi router
sys=onoff dom=onoff.9front ip=192.168.0.1

# auth server
sys=auth dom=auth.9front ether=00d059b6dac8 ip=192.168.0.2
        bootf=/386/9bootpxe

# cpu server
sys=cpu dom=cpu.9front ether=001125149137 ip=192.168.0.4
        bootf=/386/9bootpxe

# file server
sys=fs dom=fs.9front ether=001641360117 ip=192.168.0.3

# terminal
sys=x301 dom=x301.9front ether=00226811f7dd ip=192.168.0.31
        bootf=/386/9bootpxe
```


6.2.7 – Activating the changes

6.2.7.1 – NIC

Network interfaces are automatically initialized at boot time. To make a manual change
without rebooting, use the ipconfig(8) command:

```
ip/ipconfig -g 192.168.0.1 ether /net/ether0 \
        192.168.0.31 255.255.255.0
```

6.2.7.2 – cs

To refresh the network database **NOW** after changing /lib/ndb/local:

```
echo -n refresh > /net/cs
```

6.2.7.3 – dns

```
echo -n refresh > /net/dns
```

6.2.8 – Verifying network settings

```
% cat /net/ndb
ip=192.168.0.31 ipmask=255.255.255.0 ipgw=192.168.0.1
        sys=x301
        dom=x301.9front
        auth=192.168.0.2
        dns=192.168.0.1
```

6.2.8.1 – Checking routes

```
% cat /net/iproute
0.0.0.0          /96  192.168.0.1     4     none   -
192.168.0.0      /120 192.168.0.0     4i    ifc    0
192.168.0.0      /128 192.168.0.0     4b    ifc    -
192.168.0.31     /128 192.168.0.31    4u    ifc    0
192.168.0.255    /128 192.168.0.255   4b    ifc    -
255.255.255.255 /128 255.255.255.255 4b    ifc    0
```

6.2.8.1.1 – Adding static routes

Route requests for 192.168.1.0/24 through the gateway 192.168.0.99 (which itself must already be accessible via the existing network configuration):

```
echo 'add 192.168.1.0 255.255.255.0 192.168.0.99' >/net/iproute
```

Note: Manual configurations such as this may be added to optional boot scripts created in /cfg/$sysname/.

Read: ip(3)

6.2.9 – Setting up your 9front box as a forwarding gateway

Read: ip(3)

6.2.10 – Setting up aliases on an interface

Read: `ip(3)`

6.3 – How do I filter and firewall with 9front?

No.

6.4 – Dynamic Host Configuration Protocol (DHCP)

6.4.1 – DHCP client

In `/lib/ndb/local`, if no `ip=` tuple is present in the machine's definition, the boot scripts will attempt to obtain an IP address via DHCP.

To obtain a DHCP lease manually:

```
ip/ipconfig
```

Read: `ipconfig(8)`

6.4.2 – DHCP server

From `dhcpd(8)`:

Dhcpd runs the BOOTP and DHCP protocols. Clients use these
protocols to obtain configuration information. This information comes from attribute/value pairs in the network database (see ndb(6) and ndb(8)). DHCP requests are honored both
for static addresses found in the NDB and for dynamic
addresses listed in the command line. DHCP requests are
honored if either:
- there exists an NDB entry containing both the ethernet
address of the requester and an IP address on the originating network or subnetwork.
- a free dynamic address exists on the originating network
or subnetwork.

A BOOTP request is honored if all of the following are true:
- there exists an NDB entry containing both the ethernet
address of the requester and an IP address on the originating network or subnetwork.
- the entry contains a bootf= attribute
- the file in the bootf= attribute is readable.

Dynamic addresses are specified on the command line as a
list of addresses and number pairs. For example,
    ip/dhcpd 10.1.1.12 10 10.2.1.70 12
directs dhcpd to return dynamic addresses 10.1.1.12 through
10.1.1.21 inclusive and 10.2.1.70 through 10.2.1.81 inclusive.

Dhcpd maintains a record of all dynamic addresses in the
directory /lib/ndb/dhcp, one file per address. If multiple
servers have access to this common directory, they will correctly coordinate their actions.

Attributes come from either the NDB entry for the system,
the entry for its subnet, or the entry for its network. The
system entry has precedence, then the subnet, then the network. The NDB attributes used are:

ip   the IP address
ipmask the IP mask
ipgw   the default IP gateway
dom   the domain name of the system
fs   the default Plan 9 file server
auth   the default Plan 9 authentication server
dns   a domain name server
ntp   a network time protocol server
time   a time server
wins   a NETBIOS name server
www   a World Wide Web proxy
pop3   a POP3 mail server
smtp   an SMTP mail server
bootf   the default boot file; see ndb(6)

Dhcpd will answer BOOTP requests only if it has been specifically targeted or if it has read access to the boot file
for the requester. That means that the requester must specify a boot file in the request or one has to exist in NDB
for dhcpd to answer. Dhcpd will answer all DHCP requests
for which it can associate an IP address with the requester.

To configure a DHCP server on your system:

```
mkdir /lib/ndb/dhcp
```

and then modify /cfg/$sysname/cpurc or /cfg/$sysname/termrc (whichever is appropriate) to start dhcpd and tftpd at boot time:

```
ip/dhcpd
```

Read: dhcpd(8)

6.5 – PPP

Read: Dailup modem config at the Bell Labs Plan 9 wiki.

6.6 – Setting up a network bridge in 9front

Read: bridge(3) and ip(3)

6.7 – How do I boot from the network?

First, read *FQA 7.3.3 – Setting up a listener for network connections.* The file server should already be running a listener, and an auth server should already be configured and running on the network.

6.7.1 – How do I tcp boot?

It is possible to boot from local media and then mount the root file system over the network. At the bootargs prompt, type tls (the old tcp boot option will still work but is not recommended because the connection will not be encrypted). At this point, ip/ipconfig will determine network parameters using DHCP. When file (fs) or authentication (auth) server IP addresses could not be determined over DHCP then the boot process will prompt for those. When prompted for a user, enter a valid username and password that has already been configured on the auth server. The machine should then proceed to mount its root file system from the file server.

Note: Values for fs and auth may be added to plan9.ini.

Read: plan9.ini(8)

6.7.1.1 – Passing arguments to ipconfig at the bootargs prompt

When a DHCP server is not available, you may still tcp boot by configuring networking manually at the bootargs prompt. Everything after tcp! is passed as arguments to the ipconfig command.

At the prompt:

```
bootargs is (tcp, tls, il, local!device) [tcp]
```

enter something like the following:

```
tls!-g 192.168.0.1 ether /net/ether0 192.168.0.23 255.255.255.0
```
where $192.168.0.1$ is the gateway, $192.168.0.23$ is the static IP address and $255.255.255.0$ the subnet mask.

Read: `ipconfig(8)`

6.7.2 – How do I boot using PXE?

It is also possible to PXE boot a system.

On the file server, add the following lines to `/cfg/$sysname/cpurc` to start `dhcpd` and `tftpd` at boot time:
```
ip/dhcpd
ip/tftpd
```

Add an entry for `tftp` under the appropriate `ipnet=` tuple in `/lib/ndb/local`:
```
ipnet=9front ip=192.168.0.0 ipmask=255.255.255.0 ipgw=192.168.0.1
        auth=192.168.0.2
        authdom=9front
        cpu=192.168.0.4
        dns=192.168.0.1
        dnsdomain=9front
        smtp=192.168.0.4
        tftp=192.168.0.3
```

Reboot the file server:
```
fshalt -r
```

To configure machines that will PXE boot from the file server, edit `/lib/ndb/local` on the file server and add a `bootf=` (boot file) tuple to the line representing each machine:
```
sys=x301 dom=x301.9front ether=00226811f7dd ip=192.168.0.31
  bootf=/386/9bootpxe
```

For the system x301 we would then create a file `/cfg/pxe/00226811f7dd` on the file server to serve as its `plan9.ini`:
```
bootfile=/386/9pc
bootargs=tls
nobootprompt=tls
auth=192.168.0.2
fs=192.168.0.3
mouseport=ps2intellimouse
monitor=vesa
vgasize=1440x900x32
*acpi=1
user=sl
```

Note: The `user=` parameter refers to a single username that has been added both to the file server (for file permissions) as well as to the auth server (for network authentication).

If a file matching the remote system's MAC address is not found under `/cfg/pxe/`, the file `/cfg/pxe/default` (if it exists) will be used instead.

Finally, boot the desired remote systems via PXE. When prompted for a `user`, enter a valid username and password that has already been configured on the auth server. The remote system should now proceed to boot from the file server.

FQA 7 – System Management

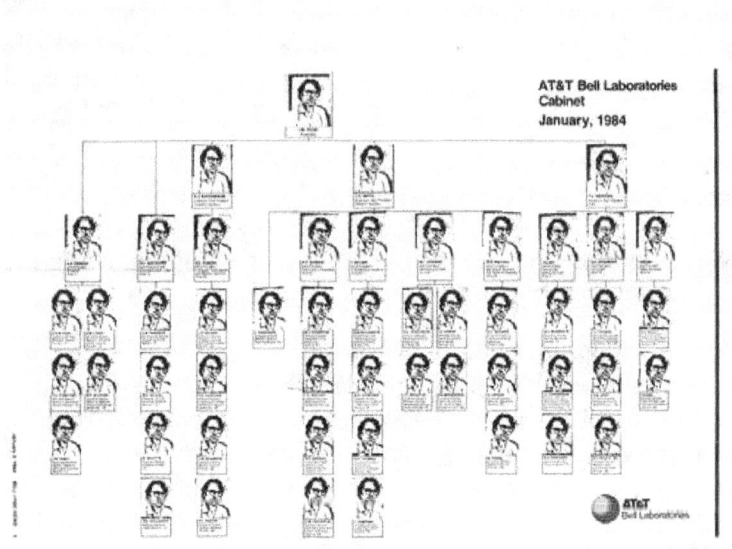

7.1 – Plan 9 Services Overview

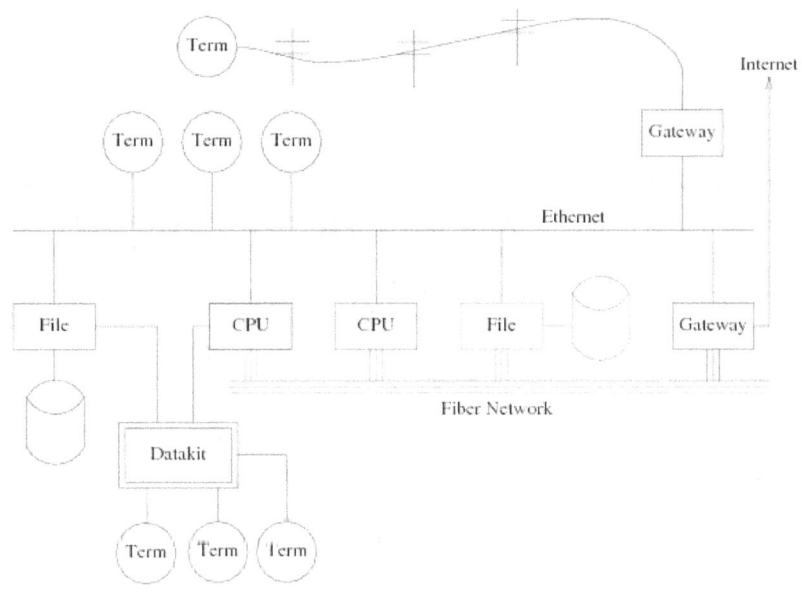

In order to be an effective system manager it is a good idea to understand how the system is designed, and how it is intended to be used.

A Plan 9 installation consists of a disk file server, an authentication server, and one or more cpu servers and terminals—all sharing the same disk file system.

That said, Plan 9 services may be run on separate machines, all together on one machine, or in various combinations. The original design of Plan 9 assumed that each network service would run on separate hardware; by design, individual components of the system are generally unaware if they co-exist on the same machine or are distributed amongst separate machines.

This document will describe individual services as if they are all running separately.

Read: *Designing Plan 9, Plan 9 From Bell Labs, The Organization of Networks in Plan 9*

7.1.1 – What is the kernel?

The kernel is a service that provides processes and resources to users active on an individual machine. Every Plan 9 machine boots a kernel.

At boot time the kernel takes on the identify of $user (the user who logs in at the console), which becomes the hostowner of the system. The hostowner in turn 1.) controls access to the kernel's resources, 2.) serves as the auth identity (authid) of the machine and the services it provides.

Note: The hostowner differs from the concept of root on a UNIX system, where a single user root may take control of all processes *and* files on the system. By contrast, even the hostowner of a Plan 9 file server cannot violate file permissions on the file server, except when permissions checking is disabled on the console or when entering special commands at the console of the file server. The hostowner controls only the *processes* running on the local machine. This fundamental separation between control of processes and file permissions is exploited throughout the Plan 9 system, but can be confusing for users coming from a UNIX background.

7.1.2 – What is the file server?

In a traditional Plan 9 network there is one disk file server, typically the only machine with a physical hard disk, that serves files to all other machines on the network. In most cases, other machines are either diskless or only use their disks for local caching. Ken Thompson's original Plan 9 file server ran a unique, special-purpose kernel that *only* served files, and whose configuration could only be changed at the console. In 9front, the file server runs a normal kernel and typically also runs as a cpu server (for remote access).

9front supports two different disk file systems for use on the file server: cwfs and hjfs. cwfs is a userspace port of Ken Thompson's original Plan 9 file server. hjfs is a new, experimental file server that stores both the cache and worm on a single partition (and thus requires less disk space to be used effectively). Both are reasonably robust.

Read: *The Plan 9 File Server* (deprecated, but partially applies to cwfs), cwfs(4), hjfs(4)

Note: Since most Plan 9 systems have no disk, security of the file server is largely protected from breaches of security in its clients. The fewer the programs that run on the file server, the more isolated it can be from security holes in programs.

Note: Users seeking access to the file server must be added as a user on the file system itself, and, if auth is enabled, added to the auth server's user database.

Note: Some users choose to run remote cpu or auth servers as stand-alone systems, each with their own local disk file systems. The distinction between all these types of systems is fuzzy and can become even fuzzier as services are enabled and disabled in different combinations.

7.1.3 – What is the auth server?

The auth server manages authentication for an entire Plan 9 network. It boots a normal kernel but is usually run on a separate, diskless machine that performs no other functions, in order to reduce the danger of a security breach compromising its kernel processes. That said, the auth server is usually also configured as a cpu server, for remote access.

Note: The cron(8) service should be run only on the auth server, where it can authenticate itself to access any of the other machines on the network.

Read: *Security in Plan 9,* auth(8)

7.1.4 – What is the cpu server?

The cpu server is used for remote computation. A cpu server's kernel runs processes in isolation, on only that machine. The boot process of a cpu server (defined as such by setting service=cpu in the machine's plan9.ini or equivalent) may be examined by reading the /rc/bin/cpurc script, which is executed at boot time. Running as a cpu server causes the kernel to adjust certain resource values that ultimately determine the behavior of the machine. For example, the cpurc script starts certain programs only if the machine is recognized as a cpu server.

Common use cases for a separate cpu server are: To execute programs compiled for a different architecture than that of the terminal; To execute programs closer to the data they are operating upon (for example, if the terminal is running over a slow link but the cpu server is on the same ethernet segment as the file server); To execute processes in physical isolation from other processes. In the early days of Plan 9, a cpu server was often significantly more powerful than the (often, special-purpose) hardware used for diskless terminals. Today, terminals are typically powerful computers in their own right, and the need for a separate machine running only as a cpu server is less common. That said, it can be useful to execute unstable or unpredictable programs on a separate machine so that frequently crashing and/or rebooting does not affect one's immediate workspace environment—especially when testing new code. In the case of remote (mail, web, etc.) servers, it is also likely that cpu access would be desired.

In practice, the disk file server, the auth server, and even some terminals will often run their own cpu listeners, to enable remote access to the processes controlled by their kernels.

Note: Users seeking access to a cpu server must first be added on the file system of the cpu server's corresponding file server (for permission to access and modify files) as well as the user database of its designated auth server (for login authentication).

Read: *The Organization of Networks in Plan 9,* cpu(1), exportfs(4)

7.1.5 – What is a terminal?

The terminal is the machine at which the Plan 9 user is most often physically located. Usually diskless, the terminal will almost always run with graphics enabled (for launching the `rio` GUI or other graphical programs). The boot process of a terminal (defined as such by setting `service=terminal` in the machine's `plan9.ini` or equivalent) may be examined by reading the `/rc/bin/termrc` script, which is executed at boot time.

Note: Many Plan 9 users run stand-alone systems that operate — effectively — as a combined terminal and file server. For example, inside a virtual machine such as qemu, or booted from hard disk on a laptop. In this case the Plan 9 network is entirely self-contained, running one kernel on one machine, which renders auth and cpu services superfluous. This configuration trades some of the inherent security of separate hardware and kernel boundaries for the convenience of combining the whole system into a single, bootable instance.

Note: Terminal users who do not run stand-alone machines or who wish to access Plan 9 network resources must first be added to the file system of the network's file server, and to the user database of the network's auth server.

7.2 – Kernel configuration and maintenance

7.2.1 – How do I mount the 9fat partition?

9front has done away with the scripts `9fat:`, `c:`, and so forth, that are found in the Bell Labs Plan 9 distribution. Instead, use the `9fs` script to mount the 9fat partition:

```
9fs 9fat
```

If you are not at the console, or if #S has not already been bound over `/dev`:

```
bind -b '#S' /dev # bind the local hard drive kernel device over /dev
9fs 9fat /dev/sdXX/9fat # specify the full path to the corresponding 9fat
```

Note: `9fs 9fat` posts a file descriptor in `/srv/dos`. If this file already exists and is already in use, `9fs 9fat` will fail. If no other process is using the file it is safe to simply remove it and run `9fs 9fat` again.

Read: `dossrv(4)`

7.2.2 – How do I modify plan9.ini?

Mount the `9fat` partition and then edit the file `/n/9fat/plan9.ini`.

Note: The file must end with a newline.

Read: `plan9.ini(8)`

7.2.3 – Kernel configuration file

Kernel configuration files are stored in the kernel directory and share the name of the kernel to which they apply. For example, the configuration file for the pc kernel is /sys/src/9/pc/pc.

7.2.4 – Kernel drivers

Kernel driver source files are located in the kernel source directory. For example, the pc kernel source is located in /sys/src/9/pc.

7.2.5 – How do I install a new kernel?

To build and install the new kernel(s) on the file system:

For 386:

```
cd /sys/src/9/pc
mk install # kernel is copied to /386/9pc
```

For amd64:

```
cd /sys/src/9/pc64
mk install # kernel is copied to /amd64/9pc64
```

For arm / bcm (Raspberry Pi, etc.):

```
cd /sys/src/9/bcm
mk install # kernel is copied to /arm/9pi2
```

For arm64 / bcm64 (Raspberry Pi 3):

```
cd /sys/src/9/bcm64
mk install # kernel is copied to /arm64/9pi3
```

For 386 and amd64 machines with local disk, it may be desired to install the new bootloader and kernels onto the 9fat partition, in order to boot directly from disk. **Note:** The bootloader needs to be continuous on disk, so simply copying over the original file does not produce the desired effect. Instead:

```
9fs 9fat
rm /n/9fat/9bootfat
cp /386/9bootfat /n/9fat/
chmod +al /n/9fat/9bootfat # defrag magic
```

then copy the desired kernels:

For 386:

```
cp /386/9pc /n/9fat/
```

For amd64:

143

```
cp /amd64/9pc64 /n/9fat/
```

Finally, if a different kernel is being intsalled than the one currently running, edit plan9.ini and change bootfile to point to the new kernel.

Read: *FQA 7.2.2 – How do I modify plan9.ini?*

7.3 – Fileserver configuration and maintenance

7.3.1 – Adding users

Add a new user on the file server:

For cwfs:

```
echo newuser username >>/srv/cwfs.cmd
```

For hjfs:

```
echo newuser username >>/srv/hjfs.cmd
```

If needed, make the new user a member of another group (example: upas):

For cwfs:

```
echo newuser upas +username >>/srv/cwfs.cmd
```

For hjfs:

```
echo newuser upas +username >>/srv/hjfs.cmd
```

Both file servers store their user database in /adm/users. Examine this file, and the contents of the /usr directory, to evaluate success.

Note: It is also possible to access the control file interactively:

For cwfs:

```
con -C /srv/cwfs.cmd
```

For hjfs:

```
con -C /srv/hjfs.cmd
```

From here commands may be entered directly.

Type Ctrl-\ to resume the con prompt, followed by q to quit.

Note: New users are created without a profile, mail directory, tmp directory (needed to edit files with sam) or other confections. To install a default profile for a new user, upon first login as that user, run:

```
/sys/lib/newuser
```

then edit `/usr/username/lib/profile` to your own specifications. The `newuser` file system command is described in the man pages `fs(8)` (for `cwfs`) and `hjfs(8)`. The default system `/lib/namespace` does the following:

```
bind -c /n/other/usr/$user/tmp /usr/$user/tmp
```

For `cwfs` users, it may be desirable to store the user's `tmp` directory on the `other` partition:

```
mkdir /n/other/usr/$user/tmp
```

7.3.2 – Configuring nvram

The cpu kernel checks the `nvram` file for valid auth credentials and attempts to copy them into `factotum` so that the machine may boot without manual intervention. To configure the `nvram`, run the command `auth/wrkey`, which will prompt for an `authid`, `authdom`, `secstore key`, and `password`. The `authid` is a synonym for the `hostowner` of the machine and should be a valid user that has already been (or will be) added to the corresponding auth server, in this case `glenda`. The `authdom` is the authentication domain for the machine, in this case `9front`. The `secstore key` and `password` are secret passwords of eight characters or more in length. The `password` is the password belonging to the `authid` user on the auth server responsible for the `authdom` entered above. The `secstore key` is the password of the user on the secure-store server (Read: *FQA 7.4.3 – secstored*). If the `secstore` client (Read: *FQA 8.4.7 – secstore*) is not being used on this machine (for example, if this is the auth server where `secstored` will run), just hit `enter` at the `secstore key:` prompt.

Run the command `auth/wrkey`:

```
bad nvram key
bad authentication id
bad authentication domain        # You may not see these errors.
authid: glenda
authdom: 9front
secstore key: [glenda's secstore password]
password: [glenda's password]
```

To ensure that the correct nvram partition is found in all cases, an `nvram` line should be added to `/n/9fat/plan9.ini`.

```
nvram=#S/YOURDRIVE/nvram
```

Note: Booting the file system with authentication enabled and an invalid `nvram` file will cause `auth/wrkey` to be run automatically at startup.

Read: `auth(8)`

7.3.3 – Setting up a listener for network connections

In order for remote machines to mount the file system of the file server, the file server must first be running a network listener. This section details the steps required to transform a terminal with disk (the result of a default install of 9front) into a disk file server for other machines.

The first step is to switch from the terminal service to the cpu service by editing the `service` line in `/n/9fat/plan9.ini`:

```
service=cpu
```

Read: *FQA 7.2.2 – How do I modify plan9.ini?*

Before rebooting, configure the nvram: *FQA 7.3.2 – Configuring nvram.* This allows the machine to load auth credentials from the `nvram` file into `factotum`, so that it can continue to boot without manual intervention.

Reboot:

```
fshalt -r
```

The next step (on cwfs; not needed on hjfs) is to enable authentication on the file server, to prevent unauthorized users from accessing the disk over the network. At the `bootargs` prompt, retype the default and add the `-c` flag to enter the file server's config mode. At the `config` prompt, type `noauth` twice to toggle authentication on the file server. Finally, type `end` to continue with the boot process:

```
bootargs is (tcp, local!device)
        [local!/dev/sdXX/fscache] local!/dev/sdXX/fscache -c
config: noauth
auth is now disabled
config: noauth
auth is now enabled
config: end
```

The machine will now continue to boot.

Once booted, the next step is to configure the file server to listen for connections from remote hosts. Modify the `bootargs` of the file server in `/n/9fat/plan9.ini`:

For cwfs:

```
bootargs=local!/dev/sdXX/fscache -a tcp!*!564
```

For hjfs:

```
bootargs=local!/dev/sdXX/fs -m 702 -A -a tcp!*!564
```

Note: The `-m 702` flag for `hjfs` allocates 702 megabytes of memory to be used as a cache. This value is typically automatically calculated by the 9front installer, and may differ on your system. There is no need to change whatever default was already configured.

Read: *FQA 7.2.2 – How do I modify plan9.ini?*

Reboot the file server:

```
fshalt -r
```

When the system finishes booting it should now be listening for network connections to the file system. Users who have been added to the file server and the auth server should now be able to authenticate and mount the file server (tcp boot, etc.).

Read: cwfs(4), hjfs(4), *FQA 6.7.1 – How do I tcp boot?*

7.3.3.1 – Stop cwfs from allowing user none to attach without authentication

```
echo nonone >>/srv/cwfs.cmd
```

7.3.3.1.1 – notes on user none

[continued on next page following]

```
/sys/src/9/port/chan.c:1321,1335
```

Date: Fri, 22 Jan 2021 15:44:05 -0800
From: Anthony Martin <ality@pbrane.org>
To: 9front@9front.org
Subject: [9front] notes on user none
Reply-To: 9front@9front.org

I remembered investigating the restrictions on user none
in the past so I went and dug out my notes. They're only
applicable to fossil and cwfs, though, so someone else
will have to go through the hjfs code to compare.

The notes are attached below.

Cheers,
  Anthony

from /sys/doc/9.ms
Finally, a special user called none has no password and is always
allowed to connect; anyone may claim to be none. None has restricted
permissions; for example, it is not allowed to examine dump files and
can read only world-readable files.

from /sys/doc/auth.ms
Factotum is the only process that needs to create capabilities, so all
the network servers can run as untrusted users (e.g., Plan 9's none or
Unix's nobody), which greatly reduces the harm done if a server is
buggy and is compromised.

kernel
- documented
    - anyone can become none with none(8)
- undocumented
    - eve can change the owner of proc(3) files to none
    - none cannot use proc(3) to view or modify the state of other processes
    - none cannot create shr(3) files on 9front

cwfs(4) and fossil(4)
- documented
    - none cannot authenticate a connection
        - auth(5) with uname "none" returns Rerror
    - none can be chaperoned on authenticated connections
        - attach(5) with afid NOFID sets uname to "none"
    - none has minimal access permissions (i.e. "world" or "other")
    - users in the "noworld" group are denied world access permissions
- undocumented
    - none cannot be a group leader
        - wstat(5) is limited

fossil(4)
- documented
    - none cannot attach to an unauthenticated connection

                                  – unless the -N flag is given to listen or srv
                          – users not in the "write" group cannot modify the file system
                                      – unless the group doesn't exist
              – undocumented
                          – none cannot modify file status information
                                  – wstat(5) returns Rerror

          # cwfs(4)
          – documented
                      – none *can* attach to an unauthenticated connection
                              – unless the nonone flag is set on 9front (undocumented)
          – undocumented
                      – none cannot attach to the dump file system
                              – attach(5) returns Rerror

7.3.4 – Mounting a file system from userspace

For cwfs:

```
# use the correct path to your fscache
% cwfs64x -n fs -f /dev/sdE0/fscache
% mount /srv/fs /n/fs
```

Note:
Running the above commands will post the file systems's console in
/srv/fs.cmd.

For hjfs:

```
# use the correct path to your fs partition
% hjfs -n hjfs -f /dev/sdE0/fs
% mount /srv/hjfs /n/hjfs
```


7.3.5 – dump

7.3.5.1 – manually trigger the dump

As hostowner,

For cwfs:

```
% echo dump >>/srv/cwfs.cmd
```

For hjfs:

```
% echo dump >>/srv/hjfs.cmd
```

7.4 – Auth server configuration and maintenance

7.4.1 – Configuring an auth server

The auth server should be booted with `service=cpu` in `plan9.ini`, and `ndb` modified to associate the new auth server with the desired `authdom`.

If the cpu server machine boots from a local disk, edit the `service` line in in `/n/9fat/plan9.ini`:

```
service=cpu
```

Read: *FQA 7.2.2 – How do I modify plan9.ini?*

If the machine boots via PXE, edit the `service` line in in the file under `/cfg/pxe/` that correspondes to its MAC address. In this case, `/cfg/pxe/000c292fd30c`:

```
service=cpu
```

Note: The contents of `/cfg/pxe/000c292fd30c` serves as the equivalent of `plan9.ini` for the PXE booted machine. Any other settings that would normally be configured in `plan9.ini` may also be entered there.

Next, `ndb` must be modified to associate the new auth server with the desired `authdom`. Assuming the auth server has a MAC address of `00:0c:29:2f:d3:0c`, an IP address of `192.168.0.2`, and a default gateway/DNS server of `192.168.0.1` that are all on the Class C network `192.168.0.0/24`, and that the `authdom` is `9front`, edit `/lib/ndb/local` and add the `authdom` and the auth server's IP under the corresponding `ipnet`:

```
ipnet=9front ip=192.168.0.0 ipmask=255.255.255.0
        ipgw=192.168.0.1
        auth=192.168.0.2 # add auth server's ip
        authdom=9front # add authdom
        fs=192.168.0.3
        cpu=192.168.0.4
        dns=192.168.0.1
        dnsdomain=9front
        smtp=192.168.0.4
```

Read: `ndb(6)`

Before rebooting, configure the nvram: *FQA 7.3.2 – Configuring nvram.* This allows the machine to load auth credentials from the `nvram` file into `factotum`, so that it can continue to boot without manual intervention.

Note: If the auth server's `hostowner` (referred to as `authid` in the `auth/wrkey` dialogue) will be any other user than the default `glenda`, that user must be authorized (in the auth context) to "speak for" other users. Assuming a hostowner of `sl`, add a rule to `/lib/ndb/auth`:

```
hostid=sl
        uid=!sys uid=!adm uid=*
```

This rule allows the user `sl` to speak for all users *except for* `sys` and `adm`.

Read: auth(8)

Reboot:

```
fshalt -r
```

At boot time, the shell script /rc/bin/cpurc consults ndb to determine if the machine is an auth server. If it is, the script will launch the keyfs process and start listeners for auth connections. If, after booting, keyfs is not running, something went wrong.

Finally, create an auth user and configure an auth password for the hostowner of the machine. This auth user should be the same name as the authid that was entered at boot time during the auth/wrkey dialogue. Likewise, set the password to match the password that was entered during the auth/wrkey dialogue. **Note:** If the user and password do not match what was entered during the auth/wrkey dialogue, users will not be able to authenticate using this auth server.

Read: *FQA 7.4.2 – Adding users*

7.4.1.1 – Avoiding an ndb entry for the auth server

It an auth server for a given authdom is not found In the local ndb, then the authdial() function from the libauthsrv library (used for resolving auth servers) will default to the dns host name p9auth.example.com, where p9auth is the sub-domain, and example.com is the authdom. This convention (where followed) is useful to avoid having to manually add auth server information for arbitrary remote networks to the local ndb.

7.4.2 – Adding users

To add a new user to the auth server, login as the auth server's hostowner, make sure auth/keyfs is running in your namespace, and then set an auth password for the user:

```
% auth/keyfs
% auth/changeuser username
Password: # type password here, will not echo
Confirm password: # confirm password here, will not echo
assign Inferno/POP secret? (y/n) n
Expiration date (YYYYMMDD or never)[return = never]:
? keys read
Post id:
User's full name:
Department #:
User's email address:
Sponsor's email address:
user username installed for Plan 9
```

Note: Questions that appear after the keys read notice are optional. Hit Enter for each one to leave them blank.

Read: auth(8), keyfs(4)

7.4.3 – secstored

Secstore authenticates to a secure-store server using a password and optionally a hardware token, then saves or retrieves a file. This is intended to be a credentials store (public/private keypairs, passwords, and other secrets) for a `factotum`.

To set up `secstored`, login to the auth server as `hostowner` and:

```
mkdir /adm/secstore
chmod 770 /adm/secstore
```

Start `secstored` at boot time by adding the following to `/cfg/$sysname/cpurc` on the auth server:

```
auth/secstored
```

Read: `secstore(1)`, `secstore(8)`

7.4.3.1 – Adding users to secstore

`secuser` is an administrative command that runs on the secstore machine, normally the auth server, to create new accounts and to change status on existing accounts. It prompts for account information such as password and expiration date, writing to `/adm/secstore/who/user` for a given secstore user.

Login to the auth server as `hostowner` and:

```
auth/secuser username
```

and answer the prompts.

By default, `secstored` warns the client if no account exists. If you prefer to obscure this information, use `secuser` to create an account `FICTITIOUS`.

Read: *FQA 8.4.7 – secstore* for more information on using the `secstore` client.

7.4.3.2 – Converting from p9sk1 to dp9ik

[continued on next page following]

Date: Wed, 6 Jan 2016 03:54:08 +0100
From: cinap_lenrek@felloff.net
To: 9front@9front.org
Subject: [9front] new factotum/authsrv/keyfs
Reply-To: 9front@9front.org

i just pushed the new code which adds dp9ik authentication support.

to update a system, the following things need to be done:

make sure you have the latest libmp/libsec
cd /sys/src/libmp; mk install
cd /sys/src/libsec; mk install

rebuild mpc (required for libauthsrv)
cd /sys/src/cmd; mk mpc.install

rebuild libauthsrv / libauth
cd /sys/src/libauthsrv; mk install
cd /sys/src/libauth; mk install

rebuild factotum/keyfs/authsrv
cd /sys/src/cmd/auth; mk install

then rebuild kernel to include the new factotum,
but dont reboot your authserver just yet
cd /sys/src/9/pc; mk install

if your /adm/keydb is still in DES format (cat it to see
if the keyfile starts with the AES signature), you need to
convert it to use the new dp9ik protocol:

make backup
cp /adm/keys /adm/keys.old
auth/convkeys -ap /adm/keys

now set the aes key in nvram (so authserver can decrypt
the keydb when it boots)
auth/wrkey

now you can reboot the AS and once its up, you have to
set new passwords for the users. logging in with the
old p9sk1 plan9 password should continue to work if
you skip this.
passwd [username]

if there are issues logging in with dp9ik because keydb
doesnt have the new key yet, you can use delkey(1) to
remove the dp9ik key from factotum as a work arround.

--

cinap

7.5 – Cpu server configuration and maintenance

7.5.1 – Configuring a cpu server

Note: Operating a cpu server requires auth services. Read: *FQA 7.4 – Auth server configuration and maintenance*

The first step in converting a terminal to a cpu server is to switch from the `terminal` service to the `cpu` service.

If the cpu server machine boots from a local disk, edit the `service` line in in `/n/9fat/plan9.ini`:

```
service=cpu
```

Read: *FQA 7.2.2 – How do I modify plan9.ini?*

If the machine boots via PXE, edit the `service` line in in the file under `/cfg/pxe/` that correspondes to its MAC address. In this case, `/cfg/pxe/000c292fd30c`:

```
service=cpu
```

Note: The contents of `/cfg/pxe/000c292fd30c` serves as the equivalent of `plan9.ini` for the PXE booted machine. Any other settings that would normally be configured in `plan9.ini` may also be entered here.

Setting `service=cpu` causes the shell script `/rc/bin/cpurc` to be run at boot time, which in turn launches a listener that scans the `/rc/bin/service` directory for scripts corresponding to various network ports. Read: `listen(8)`. The script `tcp17019` handles incoming cpu connections. Authentication for incoming cpu connections is performed by the auth server associated with the `authdom` by `ndb`. Read: *FQA 7.4.1 – Configuring an auth server*

Before rebooting, configure the nvram: *FQA 7.3.2 – Configuring nvram.* This allows the machine to load auth credentials from the `nvram` file into `factotum`, so that it can continue to boot without manual intervention.

Reboot:

```
fshalt -r
```

7.6 – Terminal configuration and maintenance

7.6.1 – Configuring a terminal

The 9front ISO boots into a livecd running the 9pc kernel, resulting in the simplest form of terminal running on the 386 architecture. A terminal may also be network booted (the preferred method) or installed to its own stand-alone file system on a local storage device.

Read: *FQA 6.7 – How do I boot from the network?*

7.6.2 – Configuring a Terminal to Accept cpu Connections

If the `hostowner` factotum has been loaded with the appropriate key and the system is listening for `cpu` connections, a user may `cpu` into a terminal that is not running auth services. To configure a terminal to accept `cpu` connections in this fashion, substitute your choice of dom (this refers to the authdom), `user` and `password`, below:

```
echo 'key proto=dp9ik dom=9front user=glenda !password=p@ssw0rd' \
        >/mnt/factotum/ctl
aux/listen1 -t 'tcp!*!rcpu' /rc/bin/service/tcp17019
```

7.6.3 – UTC Timesync

By default, `/rc/bin/termrc` sets `TIMESYNCARGS=(-rLa1000000)`, to synchronize 9front time with the real time clock. On many systems this time is saved as UTC, whereas Windows keeps the local time there. If your time is in UTC you should omit the `-L`: Put `TIMESYNCARGS=(-ra1000000)` into `/rc/bin/termrc.local`, which is executed by `/rc/bin/termrc`.

7.7 – Mail server configuration and maintenance

Incoming and outgoing mail is handled by upas and its related suite of programs. Configuration is handled by a number of files found in `/mail/lib/`, while many of upas' common functions are carried out by shell scripts that are (relatively) easy to modify.

Note: The user who runs the assorted upas programs needs read and write permissions on `/mail/queue` and `/mail/tmp`, as well as write permissions for any mailboxes where mail will be delivered.

Note: Be sure to configure proper DNS entries for your domains. If Plan 9 will host your DNS, see: *FQA 6.2.5.2 – DNS authoritative name server*

Read: *Upas – A Simpler Approach to Network Mail,* mail(1)

The following sections describe configuration of basic Internet mail services.

7.7.1 – smtpd.conf

Some changes to the default smtpd.conf are required to accept mail *for* Internet domain names, and to relay mail *for* remote hosts (most commonly, your own machines). The following lines should be changed to correspond to your network:

```
# outgoing mail will be sent from this domain by default
defaultdomain          9front.org

# do not be an open relay
norelay                on

# disable dns verification of sender domain
verifysenderdom        off

# do not save blocked messages
saveblockedmsg         off

# if norelay is on, you need to set the
# networks allowed to relay through
# as well as the domains to accept mail for
ournets 199.191.58.37/32 199.191.58.42/32 192.168.4.0/24

# domain names for which incoming mail is accepted
ourdomains 9front.org, bell-labs.co, cat-v.org
```
Read: smtpd(6), smtp(8)

7.7.2 – rewrite

To act as an Internet mail server, copy rewrite.direct to rewrite and modify to reflect your site's Internet domain name(s):

[continued on next page following]

```
# case conversion for postmaster
pOsTmAsTeR alias postmaster

# local mail
\l!(.*) alias \1
(ttr|9front.org|bell-labs.co|cat-v.org)!(.*)    alias \2
[^!@]+ translate "/bin/upas/aliasmail ´&´"
local!(.*) >> /mail/box/1/mbox

# we can be just as complicated as BSD sendmail...
# convert source domain address to a chain a@b@c@d...
@([^@!,]*):([^!@]*)@([^!]*) alias \2@\3@\1
@([^@!]*),([^!@,]*):([^!@]*)@([^!]*) alias @\1:\3@\4@\2

# convert a chain a@b@c@d... to ...d!c!b!a
([^@]+)@([^@]+)@(.+) alias \2!\1@\3
([^@]+)@([^@]+) alias \2!\1

# /mail/lib/remotemail will take care of gating to systems we don't know
([^!]*)!(.*) | "/mail/lib/qmail ´\\s´ ´net!\1´" "´\2´"
```
Read: rewrite(6)

7.7.3 – names.local

To map incoming e-mail addresses to local usernames, edit names.local accord-
ingly:

```
# postmaster goes to glenda
postmaster        glenda
```

Note: *postmaster*@[any domain] will be delivered to local user glenda.

7.7.4 – remotemail

Finally, upas needs to know what to do with mail that cannot be delivered locally. Edit
remotemail and enter the desired behavior.

To deliver mail directly to the remote server responsible for the Internet domain name in
question:

```
#!/bin/rc
shift
sender=$1
shift
addr-$1
shift
exec /bin/upas/smtp $addr $sender $*
```
Read: smtp(8)

7.7.5 – SMTP over TLS

First, make sure you have already created TLS certificates for your server.

Next, create a file `/rc/bin/service/tcp587`:

```
#!/bin/rc
user=`{cat /dev/user}
exec /bin/upas/smtpd -c /sys/lib/tls/cert -n $3
# to use with listen1, change $3 to $net
```

7.7.6 – IMAP4 over TLS

First, make sure you have already created TLS certificates for your server.

Next, create a file `/rc/bin/service/tcp993`:

```
#!/bin/rc
exec tlssrv -c/sys/lib/tls/cert -limap4d \
        -r`{cat $3/remote} /bin/ip/imap4d -p \
        -r`{cat $3/remote} >>[2]/sys/log/imap4d
        # to use with listen1, change $3 to $net
```

7.7.7 – Spam Filtering

7.7.7.1 – ratfs

From `ratfs(4)`:

> Ratfs starts a process that mounts itself (see bind(2)) on mountpoint (default /mail/ratify). Ratfs is a persistent representation of the local network configuration and spam blocking list. Without it each instance of smtpd(6) would need to reread and parse a multimegabyte list of addresses and accounts.

To configure the spam blocking list, edit `/mail/lib/blocked` as desired, according to the rules laid out in the man page. Example:

```
# allow messages from any user at 9front.org
*allow  9front.org!*

# block messages from any user at bell-labs.com
*block  bell-labs.com!*

# block messages from ip block of aol modems
block   152.166.0.0/15
```

If `ratfs` is already running, cause it to reload the modified `/mail/lib/blocked`:

```
echo reload >/mail/ratify/ctl
```

For more details, read: `ratfs(4)`, `smtpd(6)`

To launch `ratfs` at boot time, add the following line to `/cfg/$sysname/cpustart`:

```
upas/ratfs
```

and add the following line to `/lib/namespace`:

```
mount -c #s/ratify /mail/ratify
```

Note: The directory served by `ratfs` must be visible from the `upas` listener's namespace. Usually, this is accomplished by starting `ratfs` *before* the `upas` listeners.

7.7.7.2 – scanmail

Read: `scanmail(8)`

7.7.8 – Troubleshooting the mail server

An online tool that evaluates the configuration of a given mail server is available at: `https://www.mail-tester.com`

7.7.9 – Setting up a mailing list

7.7.9.1 – mlmgr

The 9front mailing lists are hosted on 9front using the `mlmgr(1)` collection of tools.

Incoming mail to a list is filtered through a custom `pipeto`, which in turn calls a script called `nml`.

Your mileage may vary.

7.8 – Web server configuration and maintenance

If you must.

7.8.1 – ip/httpd

No.

7.8.2 – rc–httpd

The `rc-httpd` web server is a simple shell script that handles static files, directory listings and drop-in CGI programs such as the werc anti-framework. `rc-httpd` is run from a file in the directory scanned by `listen(8)`, or called as an argument to `listen1(8)`.

Read: `rc-httpd(8)`

Note: `rc-httpd` is employed to serve the `9front.org` family of websites.

7.9 – TLS certificates

```
EcDSA.verify - Notepad
File  Edit  Format  View  Help
#!/bin/bash
# Verify a file with a public key using OpenSSL
# Decode the signature from Base64 format
#
# Usage: verify <file> <signature> <public_key>
#
# NOTE: to generate a public/private key use the following commands:
#
# Create the EC(DSA) Private Key
# openssl ecparam -name secp256k1 -genkey -out ec-priv.pem
# openssl ec -in ec-priv.pem -text -noout  # Display the key
#
# Extract the associated Ec(DSA) Public Key
# openssl ec -in ec-priv.pem -pubout -out ec-pub.pem
# openssl ec -in ec-pub.pem -pubin -text -noout # Display the key
#
# where <passphrase> is the passphrase to be used.


filename=$1
signature=$2
publickey=$3

if [[ $# -lt 3 ]] ; then
   echo "Usage: verify <file> <signature> <public_key>"
   exit 1
fi

base64 --decode $signiture > /tmp/$filename.sig
# the optional flag -sha256 is not needed for secp256k1 as this is the default
openssl dgst -verify $publickey -signature /tmp/$filename.sig $filename
# Clean up the system.
rm /tmp/$filename.sig

# End of script
```

To use TLS-enabled services on a Plan 9 mail server (poptls, apoptls, imaps, etc.) you need to generate a certificate and key for your mail server and tell the `factotum` of the server about that key. The following example creates a self-signed certificate:

```
ramfs -p
cd /tmp
auth/rsagen -t 'service=tls role=client owner=*' > key
chmod 600 key
cp key /sys/lib/tls/key # or: store key in secstore
auth/rsa2x509 'C=US CN=fakedom.dom' /sys/lib/tls/key | \
        auth/pemencode CERTIFICATE > /sys/lib/tls/ccrt
```

Note: Here, US is the two-digit country code, and `fakedom.dom` is the fully qualified domain name.

To load the key into the server's `factotum` at boot time, add the following line to `/cfg/$sysname/cpustart`:

```
cat /sys/lib/tls/key >>/mnt/factotum/ctl
```

Read: `rsa(8)`

FQA 8 – Using 9front

When applied consistently, simple conventions can combine to provide powerful results. In Plan 9, *conventions* are preferred to *rules*. This section explores the Plan 9 approach to actually using the computer.

8.1 – rc

> *rc was a startup script from very early times in Unix, shortened, as Ken was wont to do, from runcom, the nearest thing CTSS had to a shell—it could run up to six prespecified commands in background. The name runcom came to be applied to the scripts as well as to their interpreter.*
> — Doug McIlroy

The rc shell was written by Tom Duff for Research UNIX v10. It was later adopted as the shell for Plan 9. Some of its conventions are unusual compared with other command interpreters influenced by the Bourne shell. Although its syntax may seem strange at first, have patience; rc was designed this way on purpose. Once its (few, but powerful) features are internalized, rc simply gets out of the way.

Read: *Rc – The Plan 9 Shell,* rc(1)

8.1.1 – Prompts

Creating an rc function with the same name as your prompt allows you to easily double-click to select at the end of a previously typed line and then send it using the mouse button 2 menu (see the discussion of rio menus, below). This can be used to approximate a form of command history (see also the commands " and "", which print and execute the previous command, respectively).

Add something like this to your $home/profile:

```
fn term%{ $* }
```

In rc the ; character forces the end of a line and is treated as a noop when it appears alone, so it is also possible to create a simple prompt that would require no special prompt function in order for the prompt to be effectively ignored when selecting and sending:

```
prompt=´; ´
```

Obviously, the prompt can be named however the user sees fit.

8.1.2 – /env

Note: Contents of the /env directory are provided by the kernel and represent a separate accounting of the shell's environment; rc reads /env only on startup, and flushes/writes /env only before executing programs.

What I installed   What I expected   What I got

`rio` is the Plan 9 window system. More accurately, `rio` multiplexes input devices with and serves a file interface to a series of rectangles, inside the boundaries of which are drawn an arbitrary arrangement of pixels. Controlling the rectangles is more straightforward, and at the same time more flexible, than what is commonly expected from most "window managers."

Read: `rio(1)`, `rio(4)`

To effectively use `rio`, you need a three button mouse. If you only have a two button mouse you can emulate the middle button by holding down the `shift` key whilst pressing the right button.

Note: Button 1, 2, and 3 are used to refer to the left, middle, and right buttons respectively.

8.2.1 – The Pop-up Menu

Pressing and holding down mouse button 3 on the gray desktop or on a shell window will give you a menu with the following options:

`New`

`Resize`

`Move`

`Delete`

`Hide`

Pressing and holding down mouse button 2 on a shell window results in a menu with the following options:

cut

paste

snarf

plumb

look

send

scroll

Select an item by releasing the button over the menu item. Rio uses the same button that started an action throughout that operation. If you press another button during the action the operation is aborted and any intermediate changes are reversed.

Each menu acts as a action verb selector which then requires an object (i.e. window) to be picked to indicate which window the verb is to act on. A further mouse action may then be required.

8.2.2 – Window control

Clicking on a window brings it to the front.

You can directly change the shape of a window by clicking and dragging on the edge or corner of the window border. Mouse button 1 or 2 will allow you to drag the edge or corner to a new size, and mouse button 3 will allow you to move the window.

The mouse button 3 menu contains a list of all windows that are corrently obstructed by other windows. Selecting a label tops the window.

The pop-up menu remembers the last command chosen, so as a shortcut you can just press and release button 3 without moving the mouse between pressing and releasing to select the previous command again.

In addition, rio serves a variety of files for reading, writing, and controlling windows. Some of them are virtual versions of system files for dealing with the display, keyboard, and mouse; others control operations of the window system itself. These files, as well as the window(1) command, allow for controlling windows programmatically by reading and writing text strings. Thus simplifying the automated opening and placement of various windows with user scripts.

Read: rio(4)

8.2.3 – Text in rio windows

Text in a rio window may be freely manipulated, edited, altered, deleted and/or acted upon using either mouse chords or the options from the mouse button menus. (For an example, see the discussion of the use of `rc` prompts, above.)

The special file `/dev/text` (for the current window), or `/dev/wsys/n/text` (for window *n*) contains all text that has already appeared in the window. The contents of this file may serve as a primitive form of command history (and may be acted upon using standard command line tools), but are lost when the window is closed.

Seriously, read: `rio(4)`

8.2.4 – Scrolling

By default, a `rio` window will fill up with text and then block, obviating the need for a separate pager program (though the `p(1)` pager program still ships with the system).

Endless scrolling may be enabled by selecting `scroll` from the mouse button 2 menu.

The `up` or `down` arrow keys and `pgup` or `pgdwn` keys may be used to scroll up or down in consistently measured increments.

Holding down the `shift` key and pressing the up or down arrow key will scroll a single line in the respective direction.

9front's `rio` supports mousewheel scrolling. The heuristic employed is roughly the same as that of clicking in the scrollbar on the left of the window: when the mouse pointer is near the top of the window the scrolling increment is small, while as the mouse pointer approaches the bottom of the window the scrolling increment grows progressively larger. Presently this behavior is limited to `rio`, `sam`, and `mothra` but may later be extended to other programs.

Note: While the behavior of the arrow and page keys is fairly consistent between programs, mousewheel scrolling is not. So far, `shift`

`up` or `down` is only supported in `rio` windows.

8.2.5 – Mouse Chording

Almost anywhere — `sam(1)`, `acme(1)`, `window(1)` — you can use the following mouse chords:

`mb1` — Select text.

`mb1 double click` — Select word under cursor, or at the end/start of a line, select the whole line.

After selecting with `mb1` and while still holding `mb1` down (these chords also work with text selected by double-clicking, the double-click expansion happens when the second click starts, not when it ends):

`mb2` — Cut text.

`mb3` — Paste text (can be reverted by clicking `mb2` immediately afterwards).

To snarf (copy), click mb2 immediately followed by mb3.

8.2.6 – Keyboard Shortcuts

Almost anywhere — sam(1), acme(1), window(1) — you can use the following shortcuts:

Ctrl-u — Delete from cursor to start of line.

Ctrl-w — Delete word before the cursor.

Ctrl-h — Delete character before the cursor.

Ctrl-a — Move cursor to start of the line.

Ctrl-e — Move cursor to end of the line.

Ctrl-b — Move cursor to the position immediately after the prompt. (rio only)

Read: UNIX Keyboard Bindings

In a rio(1) window, scroll up or down one line by holding shift and pressing the up or down arrow.

8.2.7 – Color scheme

`rio` looks like this:

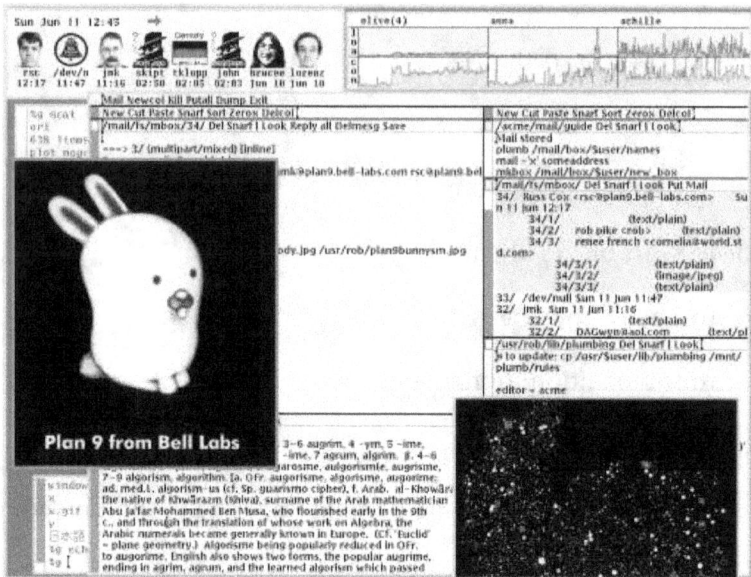

`rio`'s color scheme may be modified by editing the .c configuration files and re-compiling:

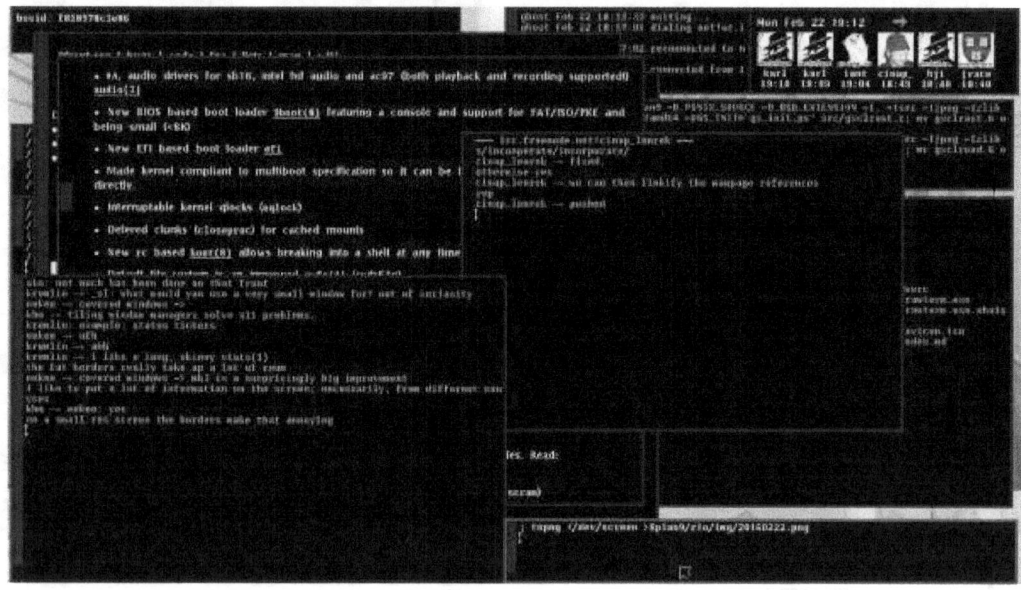

Note: Someone will mock you for doing this.

See: http://plan9.stanleylieber.com/rio, https://ftrv.se/14

Rob Pike, rio's author, was all like:

> the clean appearance of the screen comes mostly from laziness, but the color scheme is (obviously) deliberate. the intent was to build on an observation by edward tufte that the human system likes nature and nature is full of pale colors, so something you're going to look at all day might best serve if it were also in relaxing shades. renee french helped me with the specifics of the color scheme (she's a professional illustrator and my color vision is suspect), once i'd figured out how i wanted it to look. there are still some features of the color system that i put in that i think no one has ever noticed. that's a good thing, in my opinion; the colors should fade away, if you'll pardon the expression. having used other systems with different approaches to color screens, most especially windows XP (extra pukey), i think tufte was right.

Rob Pike, 2003

> The color scheme was an attempt to honor a point made originally in a little brochure by Edward Tufte that the colors of nature are soft and quiet and peaceful to look at, while most computer screens are covered in glaring bright colors. When color came to the system I wanted it to be pleasant.

Rob Pike, 2008

See: edwardtufte.com

8.2.8 – Why is rio like this?

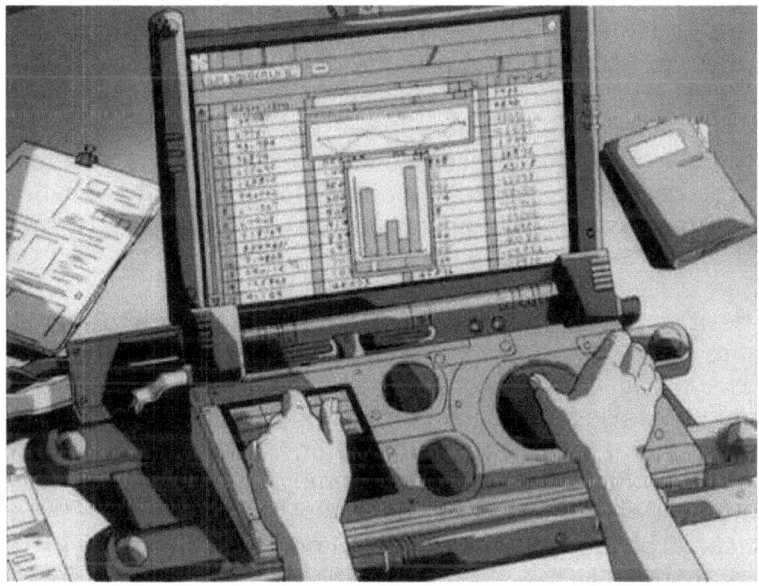

Window systems should be transparent. That's the argument put forward in the famous paper by rio's author, Rob Pike.

Do you have a mouse?

Click here to find out!

Beyond this, Rob offered an explanantion (in response to a question on the 9fans mailing list) of some of the choices made in the design of 8½ and `rio`:

> functioning cursor keys would still be a speed benefit.

This feels true but is false. There were some fascinating experiments done a few years ago in which people were given a long, tedious editing task. Some of the people were keyboard fans, some were mouse fans. Both folks were asked to do the task two ways, in random order, once using the mouse to do the editing, once using cursor keys etc. Regardless of their predilections, which was stated up front, after the experiment everyone who did the task agreed that it was faster to use the keyboard than the mouse to complete the task. Everyone. Here's the kicker: everyone was wrong. They were being timed, and in fact the reverse was true. Although they thought the keyboard was faster, doing the task using the mouse was faster for everyone, by a substantial fraction.

The explanation, besides the obvious that arrow keys are actually pretty slow if you're going more than a line or character, is that people feel the mouse wastes time because you need to grab it and move it, but it's time well spent. The part of the brain that uses keyboard commands to move the cursor is a higher-order function, and thinking and planning how to use the keys to get to the destination blocks thinking about the editing task at hand. But using the mouse is done by a lower-order part of the brain, which keeps the editing part of the brain clear. There's less task switching going on when you use the mouse, so you work more efficiently.

If you don't believe me, the story is here:

http://www.asktog.com/readerMail/1999-12ReaderMail.html

Thanks to some forgotten 9fan who mentioned this a while back. I didn't know about these experiments when I said, long ago, that using arrow keys to

170

point at a display is like telling someone how to go somewhere by giving directions, while using a mouse is like pointing at a map. In fact, I never used a screen editor until I had a mouse, for just this reason.

Rob Pike, 2001

8.2.9 – tips

8.2.9.1 – Taking a screenshot

To capture the entire screen:

```
topng </dev/screen >screen.png
```

To capture only the current window:

```
topng </dev/window >window.png
```

It is also possible to capture *other* windows:

```
topng </dev/wsys/n/window >window.png
```

where *n* is the number of the window being captured.

Read: `rio(4)`

8.2.9.2 – Prevent console messages from overwriting the screen

To capture console messages in a `rio` window, open a new window and:

```
cat /dev/kprint
```

8.3 Text Editors

8.3.1 – sam

The text editor `sam` was created by Rob Pike, and included in Research UNIX V9 (circa 1986), and later included with Plan 9.

See: http://sam.cat-v.org

Read:

The Text Editor sam — The original paper by Rob Pike.

A Tutorial for the Sam Command Language — Documents the editing language.

sam quick reference card

`sam(1)` man page

Dan Flavin, *Document for Untitled (to the "innovator" of Wheeling Peachblow),* 1968

8.3.1.1 – Scrolling

9front's slightly modified version of `sam` supports mousewheel scrolling in the same manner as `rio`.

Read: *FQA 8.2.4 – Scrolling*

8.3.1.2 – Mouse Chording

9front `sam` supports the same mouse chording as `rio`.

Read: *FQA 8.2.5 – Mouse Chording*

8.3.1.3 – Why does sam have a separate snarf buffer from rio?

The program's author, Rob Pike, says:

> was a consequence of running over 1200 baud when sam was first written. you didn't want every cut and paste to bounce off the remote end at that speed. nowadays that argument has less weight. on the other hand, i still kinda like that you can have an editing session that doesn't corrupt what you have in rio's snarf buffer. i tried the unified way in acme and i often (not always) miss the old way.

Rob Pike, 2003

8.3.1.4 – Keyboard Shortcuts

`Esc` — Cut (and consequently, snarf) the selected text.

`Ctrl-b` — Switch focus to the edit window.

8.3.2 – acme

> *There is also an alternative user interface, acme(4), that some people use as their editor.*
> — Geoff Collyer

The text editor acme was created by Rob Pike. It builds on the sam command language, and adds new features, which have proven very popular.

See:

http://acme.cat-v.org

The Acme Readme

Acme: A User Interface for Programmers — The original paper by Rob Pike.

acme(1) — Commands: acme, win, awd, interactive text windows.

acme(4) — The file system interface: control files for text windows.

A Tour Of Acme — Video tutorial by Russ Cox explaining the main features and principles of Acme.

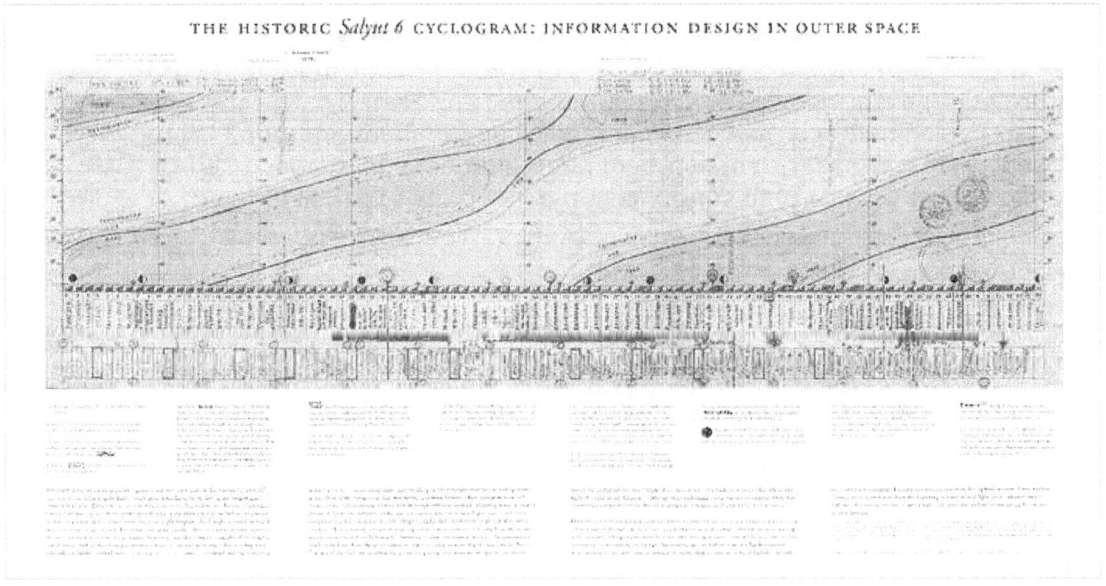

Handmade cyclogram by Russian cosmonaut, Georgi Grechko.

8.4 – Internet

Sending and receiving bits via alien protocols.

8.4.1 – Mail

Read: `mail(1)`, *FQA 7.7 – Mail server configuration and maintenance*

8.4.1.1 – upasfs

From `upasfs(4)`:

> Fs is a user level file system that caches mailboxes and presents them as a file system. A user normally starts fs in his/her profile after starting plumber(4) and before starting a window system, such as rio(1) or acme(1). The file system is used by nedmail(1), acme(1)'s mail reader, and imap4d and pop3 (both pop3(8)) to parse messages. Fs also generates plumbing messages used by biff and faces(1) to provide mail announcements.

Read: `upasfs(4)`, `pop3(8)`, `faces(1)`

8.4.1.1.1 – Reading gmail via IMAP

```
upas/fs -f /imaps/imap.gmail.com/your.username@gmail.com
```

The first time this command is run, you should see an error that looks something like this:

```
upas/fs imap: server certificate 22471E10D5C1E41768048EF5567B27F532F33
        not recognized
upas/fs: opening mailbox: bad server certificate
```

To add this certificate to your system, type:

```
echo ´x509 sha1=22471E10D5C1E41768048EF5567B27F532F33´ \
        >>/sys/lib/tls/mail
```

Once upas/fs is running, you can open as many additional gmail mailboxes (labels) as you wish:

```
echo open /imaps/imap.gmail.com/your.username@gmail.com/yourlabel \
        yourlabel >/mail/fs/ctl
```

Note: Opening large mailboxes over a slow 9p link will be very slow.

8.4.1.1.2 – Sending mail with gmail

Add your gmail password to the factotum:

```
echo 'key proto=pass server=smtp.gmail.com service=smtp \
        user=your.username@gmail.com !password=yourpassword'\
        >/mnt/factotum/ctl
```

Modify /mail/lib/remotemail to gateway mail through your gmail account:

```
#!/bin/rc
shift
sender=your.username@gmail.com
shift
addr=tcp!smtp.gmail.com!587
shift
fd=`{/bin/upas/aliasmail -f $sender}
switch($fd){
case *.*
        ;
case *
        fd=gmail.com
}
exec /bin/upas/smtp -u your.username@gmail.com -a -h $fd $addr $sender $*
```

Before this will work you need to retrieve the certificate hash. This can be done by trying to send an e-mail and then looking for the hash in the log:

```
echo hello | mail -s test your.username@gmail.com
```

Then look in /sys/log/smtp for the following error:

```
cert for smtp.gmail.com not recognized:
        sha256=wnu7Uuzq4MlyJHP90+8f2smoh6x3cj0dG5z02jJ1X42
```

Add the certificate to your system:

```
echo 'x509 sha256=wnu7Uuzq4MlyJHP90+8f2smoh6x3cj0dG5z02jJ1X42' \
        >> /sys/lib/tls/smtp
```

You should now be able to send e-mail through gmail! I'm sorry.

Note: This configuration breaks local e-mail delivery.

8.4.1.2 – nedmail

`nedmail` is a command line mail client similar to the classic mail client shipped with Research UNIX.

Read: `nedmail(1)`

8.4.1.2.1 – mother

`mother` is a clone of `nedmail`, written in `rc`. It offers some convenient new features and is easy to extend.

Download it here: http://plan9.stanleylieber.com/mother/

8.4.1.2.2 – Nail

`Nail` is a clone of acme's `Mail`, written in c. It offers some convenient new features.

Update: `Nail` has been renamed `Mail` and integrated into `acme` to replace the original `Mail`. Just type `Mail` to use `Nail`.

8.4.1.3 – nupas

Read: *Scaling Upas*, by Erik Quanstrom **Note:** Erik's nupas has been merged with 9front's upas.

8.4.2 – NNTP

Read: `newt(1)`, `nntpfs(4)`

8.4.3 – IRC

8.4.3.1 – ircrc

`ircrc` is an IRC client implemented in `rc`. It is included with 9front.

Read: `ircrc(1)`

8.4.3.2 – irc7

A persistent IRC client was written in the c programming language by Andrey Mirtchovski. It has been modified slightly by 9front users (mainly, adding an −e flag to the `ircsrv` program that implements SSL connections).

8.4.3.3 – ircs

A persistent IRC client was written in the c programming language by jpm. Inspired by irc7.

8.4.3.4 – wircrc

A windowed version of `ircrc` was implemented in rc by cinap_lenrek. Several unsanctioned versions with various additions have since occasionally been spotted.

8.4.4 – FTP

Read: `ftpfs(4)`

8.4.5 – HTTP

8.4.5.1 – mothra

mothra is the standard web browser. It is a trivial program written in 1995 by Tom Duff. It ignores Javascript, CSS and many HTML tags. It was dropped from Plan 9 after the 2nd Edition, but has been picked up and (somewhat) refined for 9front. mothra now uses webfs, and no longer supports non-HTTP protocols.

Read: mothra(1), webfs(4)

8.4.5.2 – abaco

no.

8.4.5.3 – hget

hget is a command line HTTP client (similar to programs such as curl or wget) that started out as a c program in Plan 9 from Bell Labs, but was re-implemented in rc for 9front. hget now uses webfs and no longer supports non-HTTP protocols.

Read: hget(1), webfs(4)

8.4.5.4 – charon

The Inferno operating system can be run hosted on Plan 9, and includes a GUI web browser called charon, which implements ECMASCRIPT 1.0 as well as additional HTML attributes.

Note: charon is ancient and is not really a sufficient replacement for 9front's web browsers. The rudimentary javascript support can be useful for some simple tasks.

8.4.5.5 – i

There exists an unfinished/buggy port of charon from Inferno's limbo programming language to Plan 9 c.

8.4.5.6 – NetSurf

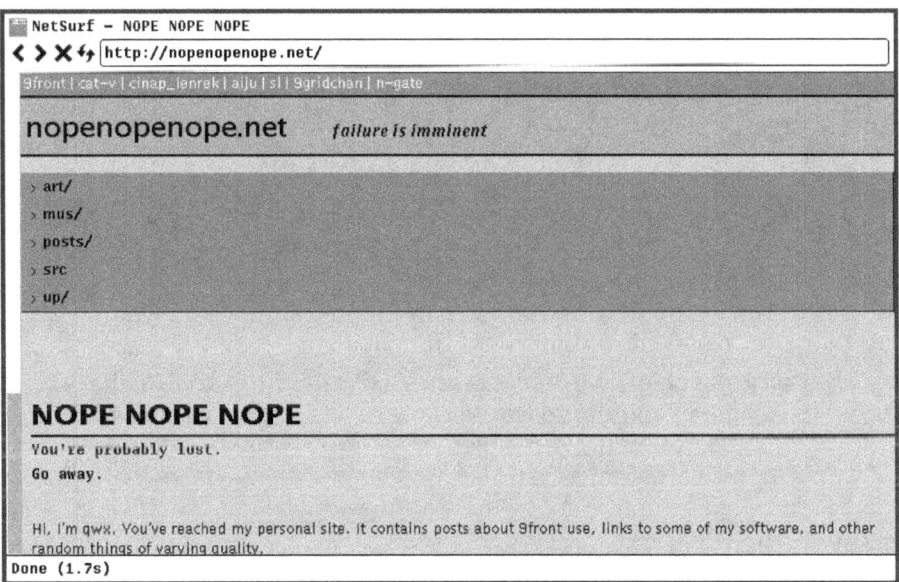

NetSurf has been ported to Plan 9 (APE + native frontend). It nearly works.

Download it here: https://github.com/netsurf-plan9/nsport

8.4.6 – SSH

Several SSH clients exist for Plan 9, none of which are perfect.

8.4.6.1 – ssh

9front used to ship with the original Plan 9 native SSH1 client from Bell Labs. It has since been replaced with a new SSH2 client that has been written from scratch. The new client supports only chacha20-poly1305 cipher and curve25519 Diffie-Hellman for key exchange. RSA public key and password authentication are supported with factotum.

Read: ssh(1)

8.4.6.1.1 – sshfs

9front ships with an sshfs client that implements the SFTP protocol over the existing ssh(1) client.

Read: sshfs(1)

8.4.6.1.2 – sshnet

Outgoing and incoming TCP connections can be proxied to an SSH server using the sshnet(4) filesystem.

Read: Free Carrots #1: VNC over SSH

8.4.6.2 – ssh2

Programmers at Coraid created a Plan 9 native SSH2 client that was picked up (and completely rewritten) by Bell Labs. It is currently not included with 9front.

Note: There are bugs and expected features are missing. Consult the source.

8.4.6.3 – scpu

Two 9front users (taruti and mischief) worked on an SSH2 client written in the Go programming language. It has been extended to work with Plan 9 factotum(4), but still does not fully honor complex Plan 9 dial(2) strings.

8.4.6.3.1 – Public Key Authentication

The scpu command can be configured to use public key authentication:

```
auth/rsagen -t 'service=ssh' >$home/lib/ssh/key
auth/rsa2ssh -2 $home/lib/ssh/key >$home/lib/ssh/key.pub
# must be present before running scpu
cat $home/lib/ssh/key >/mnt/factotum/ctl
```

Then add the contents of $home/lib/ssh/key.pub to $HOME/.ssh/authorized_keys on the remote host.

Note: This same key may be used for multiple hosts.

8.4.6.4 – OpenSSH

Plan 9 user fgb ported OpenSSH 4.7p1, OpenSSL 0.9.8g 19 Oct 2007 to Plan 9. It is available in his contrib directory (on the Bell Labs server), or a 386 binary is available here (to install, unpack it over /): openssh.tgz.

8.4.6.5 – sftpfs

An implementation of sftpfs was created for Plan 9 that can work with either the native SSH clients or fgb's OpenSSH port.

8.4.6.5.1 – Mounting a remote u9fs share over SSH

The u9fs program runs on UNIX and serves an unencrypted 9P(2) share. It is possible to mount such a share over SSH.

With ssh:

```
srv -s 5 -e 'ssh -u sl -h wm ''/usr/local/bin/u9fs \
        -u sl -na none''' wm /n/wm
```

With ssh2:

```
srv -s 5 -e 'ssh2 -l sl wm ''/usr/local/bin/u9fs \
        -u sl -na none''' wm /n/wm
```

With scpu:

```
srv -s 5 -e 'scpu -u sl -h wm -c \
        ''/usr/local/bin/u9fs -u sl -na none''' wm /n/wm
```

In all cases, an SSH connection is opened to remote UNIX host wm, logged in with user sl and mounted on Plan 9 under /n/wm.

Read: u9fs(4), srv(4)

8.4.7 – secstore

Typing in lots of passwords over and over again is annoying.

Secstore authenticates to a secure-store server using a password and optionally a hardware token, then saves or retrieves a file. This is intended to be a credentials store (public/private keypairs, passwords, and other secrets) for a factotum.

Read: *FQA 7.4.3 – secstored* for information on setting up the secstore server, and: *FQA 7.4.3.1 – Adding users to secstore* to add users.

Once a user has been added to secstored, the user may add to the file read by factotum at startup. To do so, open a new window and type

```
% ramfs -p; cd /tmp
% auth/secstore -g factotum
secstore password: [user's secstore password]
% echo 'key proto=apop dom=x.com user=ehg !password=hi' >> factotum
% auth/secstore -p factotum
secstore password: [user's secstore password]
% read -m factotum > /mnt/factotum/ctl
```

and delete the window. The first line creates an ephemeral memory-resident workspace, invisible to others and automatically removed when the window is deleted. The next three commands fetch the persistent copy of the secrets, append a new secret, and save the updated file back to secstore. The final command loads the new secret into the running factotum.

The ipso command packages this sequence into a convenient script to simplify editing of files stored on a secure store. It copies the named files into a local ramfs and invokes ditor on them. When the editor exits, ipso prompts the user to confirm copying modifed or newly created files back to secstore. If no file is mentioned, `ipso` grabs all the user's files from secstore for editing.

By default, `ipso` will edit the secstore files and, if one of them is named factotum, flush current keys from `factotum` and load the new ones from the file.

Read: `secstore(1)`, `secstore(8)`

8.4.8 – drawterm

`drawterm` is a program that users of non–Plan 9 systems can use to establish graphical cpu connections with Plan 9 cpu servers. Just as a real Plan 9 terminal does, `drawterm` serves its local name space as well as some devices (the keyboard, mouse, and screen) to a remote cpu server, which mounts this name space on `/mnt/term` and starts a shell. Typically, either explicitly or via the profile, one uses the shell to start `rio`. The original version is effectively abandoned, but is available here: `http://swtch.com/drawterm`

There also exists a fork of Russ Cox's drawterm that incorporates features from 9front, most importantly DP9IK authentication support (see `authsrv(6)`) and the TLS based `rcpu(1)` protocol: `http://drawterm.9front.org`.

Note: The fork is the preferred version of drawterm for use with 9front because the old auth protocol is considered deprecated and the old CPU listeners are now disabled by default.

Pending integration of article from: `http://wiki.9front.org/drawterm`

8.4.8.1 – Connect to Plan 9 from a mobile device

Use an SSH client to connect to a remote UNIX SSH server that can run the 9front fork's `drawterm -G`:

`http://helpful.cat-v.org/Blog/2017/11/29/0/`

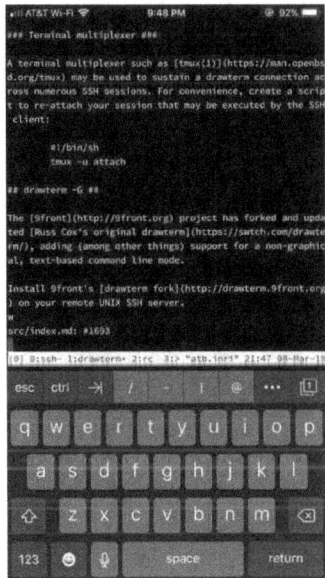

8.4.8.2 – drawterm behind firewalls

`drawterm` connects to the cpu service, which normally listens on TCP port 17019, after authenticating against the auth server, which normally listens on TCP port 567. Authentication against the auth server is bypassed when connecting as the auth server's hostowner.

On the occassion you find yourself behind a firewall that blocks the auth/ticket TCP port 567, or the cpu TCP port 17019, you can configure your auth or cpu servers to listen on different ports.

To configure the auth server to listen on TCP port 80, in addition to TCP port 567:

```
cd /bin/service.auth
cp tcp567 tcp80
```

From your command line, or script, use Plan 9 dial strings:

```
drawterm -a tcp!<auth_server>!80 -h <cpu_server> -u <username>
```

example:

```
drawterm -a tcp!auth.9front.org!80 -h cpu.9front.org -u ken
```

To configure your cpu server to listen on a different port:

```
cd /rc/bin/service
cp tcp17019 tcp23
```

From your command line:

```
drawterm -a tcp!auth.9front.org!80 -h tcp!cpu.9front.org!23 -u ken
```

This will attempt to connect to your auth server on TCP port 80 (HTTP) and to your cpu server on TCP port 23 (Telnet).

Note: The same use of Plan 9 dial strings works for specifying auth servers on Plan 9 VMs behind firewalls. Use the dial string for auth in `/lib/ndb/local`: `auth=tcp!<auth_server>!80`

Read: `listen(8)`, `authsrv(6)`, `dial(2)`

8.4.9 – Peer to Peer (P2P)

You know what we mean.

8.4.9.1 – Tinc

`tinc` implements the mesh peer to peer VPN protocol from `https://www.tinc-vpn.org/` as of version 1.0.32.

Read: `tinc(8)`

8.4.9.2 – Torrents

8.4.9.2.1 – ip/torrent

Native client. Works great. Does not support magnet links.

Read: `torrent(1)`

8.4.9.2.2 – torrent

Client written in Go. Works great. Supports magnet links.

Download it here: `https://github.com/anacrolix/torrent`

8.5 – Audio

Pending integration of article at `http://nopenopenope.net/posts/audio`

Thanks, qwx!

Meanwhile, read: `audio(1)`, `audio(3)`

Use: `play(1)`, `zuke(1)`

8.6 – External Media

8.6.1 – Mount an ISO9660 CD-ROM

```
mount <{9660srv -s} /n/iso /dev/sdD1/data # cd-rom drive
```

or:

```
mount <{9660srv -s} /n/iso /path/to/9front.iso
```

Read: dossrv(4)

8.6.2 – Burn a CD-ROM

```
cdfs
cp 9front.iso /mnt/cd/wd
rm /mnt/cd/wd
```

Read: cdfs(4)

8.6.3 – Mount a FAT formatted USB device

FAT formatted USB devices are automatically mounted under the /shr directory.

Note: Devices must be FAT or FAT32 formatted; exFAT is not supported.

8.7 – Emulation

8.7.1 – Linux Emulation

`linuxemu` is a program that can execute Linux/i386 ELF binaries on Plan 9. Semi-modern web browsers and other Linux programs may be run using `linuxemu` (if necessary, in conjunction with the `equis` X11 server).

Note: `linuxemu` can only be run on a Plan 9 system booted with a 386 kernel and binaries.

BOOTSTRAP

To run `linuxemu`, you need a Linux root file system packed into a tarball:

http://felloff.net/usr/cinap_lenrek/mroot-linuxemu.tbz

http://plan9.stanleylieber.com/linuxemu/mroot.tgz

The `mroot-linuxemu.tbz` version contains no symlinks and can be extracted with plain Plan 9 tools `bunzip` and `tar`.

The `mroot.tgz` version contains the same Debian Sarge base as `mroot-linuxemu.tbz`, but with several additional packages pre-installed:

9base

dmenu-4.1.1

dwm-5.8.2

gcc 3.3.5

linux-kernel-headers

mercurial 0.9.4

opera 10.11

python 2.3.5

xlib-dev

and more.

You can create your own `mroot` with `debootstrap` on Debian Linux, or help write an installer that unpacks and installs an alternative distribution on Plan 9... In any case, `linuxemu` is not hardwired to any Linux distribution!

RUNNING

Use the provided `linux` script to chroot into your Linux `mroot`. The `linux` script is neccesary because for Linux programs to run, shared libraries from your `mroot` have to appear in its `/lib` and `/usr/lib` directories, while configuration files are expected to be in `/etc`. The script will build a private namespace and then bind the Linux `mroot` over the Plan 9 root. The original Plan 9 namespace is mounted within `linuxemu` under `/9`.

Assuming `mroot` is located in the current directory, start `linuxemu` like this:

```
linux -r ./mroot /bin/bash -i
```

If the `-r` option is omitted, the Linux `mroot` defaults to `/sys/lib/linux` on the Plan 9 machine.

In the Linux `mroot`, `/etc/resolv.conf` should be changed to match your network nameserver. In addition, `/etc/apt/sources.list` should be updated to a working Debian mirror. Sarge packages can still be accessed at:

```
deb   http://archive.debian.org/debian-archive/debian   sarge
main
```

EXAMPLES

Linux X11 programs may be used in conjunction with the `equis` X11 server. For example, to run the Opera web browser under your Linux `mroot`, start `equis` in a `rio` window, start `linuxemu` in another `rio` window and then from within `linuxemu`:

```
dwm & # X11 window manager
opera & # web browser
```

Opera should (eventually) appear in the `equis` window. A window manager (this example uses dwm) is recommended so that X11 programs interact with window resources properly.

DEBUGGING

If `linuxemu` crashes, use acid to figure out whats going on:

```
mk acid
acid -l linuxemu.acid <pid>
```

Then you can issue the following commands:

```
ustk()
```

dump a (userspace) stacktrace for the current thread:

```
umem(Current())        dump the memory mappings
ufds(Current())        dump the filedescriptor table
utrace(Current())      dump the internal tracebuffer
                       (enabled by -d option)
```

Use `xasm()` and `xcasm()` for disassembly for Linux code.

Read: `acid(1)`

You can also enable full trace logging:

```
linux -r ./mroot -dd /bin/bash -i >[2]/tmp/linuxemu.log
```

This slows `linuxemu` down considerably. In case of race conditions, it often happens that the bug disapears when doing full trace logging!

8.7.2 – Nintendo

Emulators for several Nintendo video game consoles ship with the system:

gb — Game Boy

gba — Game Boy Advance

nes — Nintendo Entertainment System

snes — Super Nintendo Entertainment System

Read: `nintendo(1)`

8.7.3 – Sega

An emulator for the Sega Megadrive/Genesis video game console ships with the system:

md — Sega Mega Drive/Genesis

Read: `sega(1)`

8.7.4 – Commodore

An emulator for the Commodore 64 home computer ships with the system:

 c64 — Commodore 64

Read: `commodore(1)`

8.7.5 – PC

An emulator for PC compatible computers ships with the system:

 vmx — virtual PC

Read: vmx(1), vmx(3)

8.7.5.1 – Virtualization Using vmx(1)

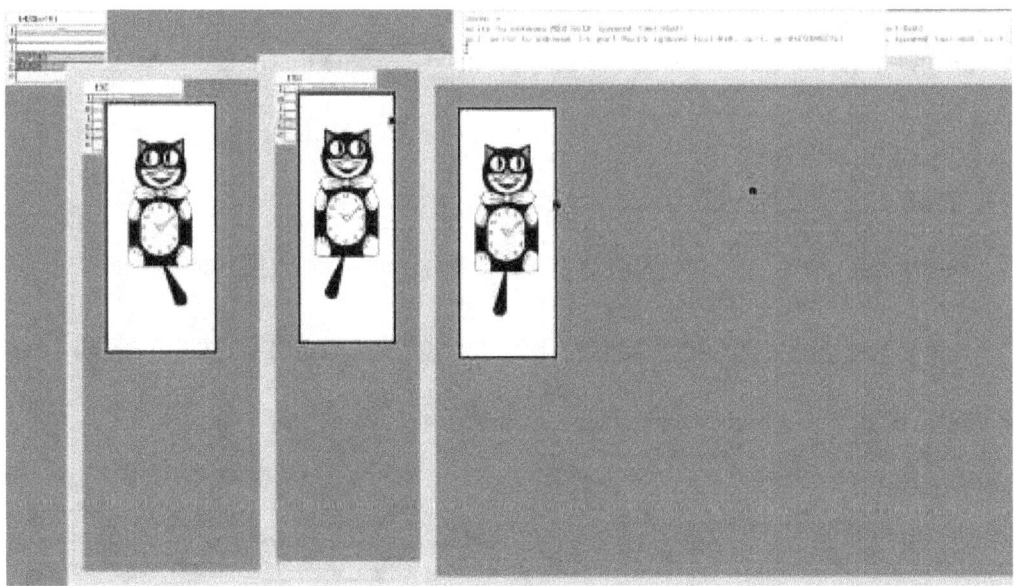

vmx(1) simulates a virtual PC running a specified kernel file, by using virtualization extensions found on recent intel processors. Currently, only 9front and recent Linux and OpenBSD kernels are supported.

The virtual PC is configured on vmx(1)'s command line, and the hardware specified is seen as virtio devices. It will use one of the host's CPU cores, and will run on the same architecture as the host.

Note: vmx executes the operating system's kernel directly, acting as a bootloader. It therefore needs explicit support for it unless the kernel is in multiboot format.

Note: vmx currently works on intel processors only, and requires a number of virtualization features. To check if your processor is supported, use icanhasvmx(8).

Basic examples:

- Boot 386 kernel with 1 GB of RAM, a 9front iso as a disk, a network interface through ether0 and a 640x480 framebuffer:

```
vmx -M 1G -d 9front.iso -n ether0 -v 640x480 /386/9pc
```

- Instead of a framebuffer, use con(1) to connect to the console:

```
window -scroll 'bind ''#|'' /n/p; \
        <>[3]/n/p/data1 {echo 3 >/srv/pipe; \
        con -r /n/p/data}'
vmx -c /srv/pipe -M 1G -d 9front.iso /386/9pc 'console=0'
```

8.7.5.1.1 Block Devices

It may be desirable to attach a disk to the virtual PC. One may then specify a number of files to be used as raw disk images with the −d flag. The files may be virtually anything so long as vmx(1) can overwrite them.

The common options here include plain files, sd(3) disks, or ISO images.

The fastest way to generate a big plain file is to create a sparse file. For example, to create a 4 GB sparse file with dd(1):

```
dd </dev/zero −of dicks −bs 1 −count 1 \
        −seek '{echo 4*1024*1024*1024−1 | pc −n}
```

Using a real disk might yield somewhat faster performance. For example, using a USB:

```
vmx −d 9front.iso −d /dev/sdUxxxxx/data −v 640x480 /386/9pc
```

Use real disks with caution! vmx may induce kernel panics in the guest, for instance through bugs or quirks in the virtio devices' implementation. Beware that the host crashing may also trash your disks -- for instance, giving the guest too much memory, which is always allocated in full on start up, will trigger an OOM on the host.

8.7.5.1.2 Ethernet

If network connectivity is required, the −n parameter specifies an interface to bridge as a virtio ethernet card. vmx(1) will then send and receive traffic on this interface like the host. Wireless ethernet interfaces may also be used without any additional work. The interface can also be a dial string or a plain file. The emulated card's MAC address is random by default, and can be changed using an optional ea: prefix.

For example, to bridge an ethernet interface and use DE:AD:BE:EF:CA:FE for the virtio device's MAC:

```
vmx −d 9.img −n ea:deadbeefcafe!ether0 −v 640x480 /386/9pc
```

8.7.5.1.3 OpenBSD

OpenBSD kernels may change radically between releases. Only 6.1 and later have been tested. Keep in mind that the versions of the kernel passed to vmx(1) and the system provided on a disk must be in sync.

Besides the various kernel files and optional devices, little is needed to coerce OpenBSD to work.

To use the OpenBSD installer, first find a bsd.rd kernel. To then use an existing OpenBSD install, use a bsd kernel instead. A networked install may be used if an ethernet interface is specified on the command line: it will use OpenBSD's vio(4) driver. Otherwise, an install??.fs file may be used as a disk.

Note: OpenBSD/386 does not support plain framebuffer graphics. You would need to either use VESA, or configure a COM device and add a `tty=` option to the command line.

For example, to install OpenBSD 6.2 to a disk file using an install image and VESA graphics:

```
vmx -d obsd.img -d install62.fs -v vesa:640x480 bsd.rd
```

Boot options are given as the kernel's command line. The root device is specified with the `device=` option, and if unset, is queried by OpenBSD's bootloader.

To use VESA with X11, one must specify the -v argument with a vesa: prefix, one or more display modes, and set `machdep.allowaperture=2`.

Example usage:

```
vmx -M 1G -c /srv/pipe -n ether0 -d /dev/sdUa2595/data \
    -v vesa:640x480,800x600,1024x768 \
    bsd ´tty=com0´ ´device=sd0a´ ´db_console=on´
```

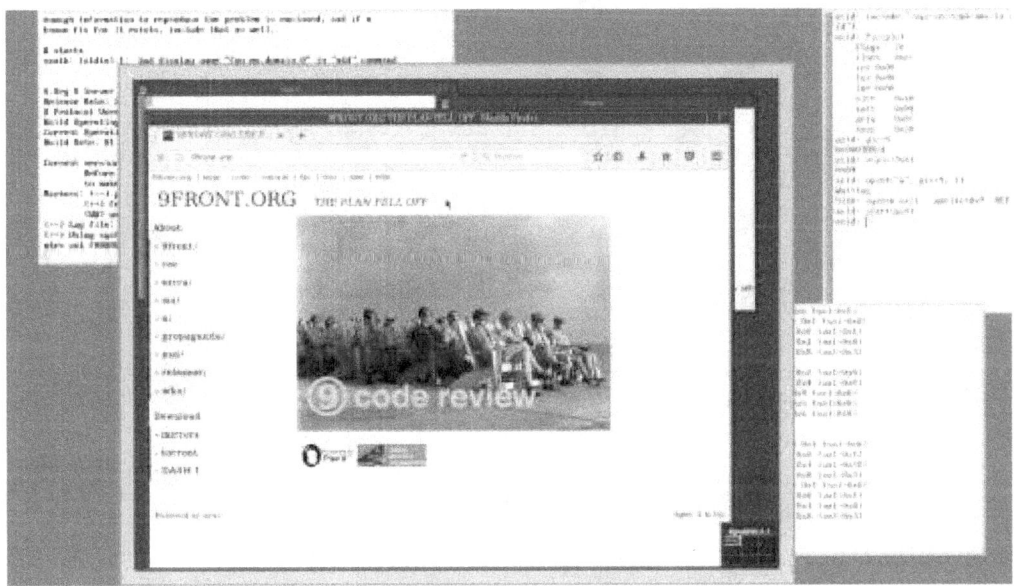

8.7.5.1.4 Linux

You will need both a kernel and an initrd which will be used as a module. You must also specify the root disk on the kernel's command line. The most convenient way to obtain a kernel is to extract it from the ISO; read `9660srv(4)`

An example with Alpine Linux:

193

```
vmx -M 1G -n ether0 -d alpine-standard-3.6.2-x86_64.iso \
       -d alp.img -m initramfs-hardened -v vesa:800x600 \
       vmlinuz-hardened
```

After installation:

```
vmx -M 1G -n ether0 -d alp.img \
       -m initramfs-hardened -v vesa:800x600 \
       vmlinuz-hardened ´root=/dev/vda1´
```

Recent versions of Alpine Linux might require specifying the `rootfstype=` parameter. Typically, its value will be `ext4`.

8.7.5.1.5 Windows NT

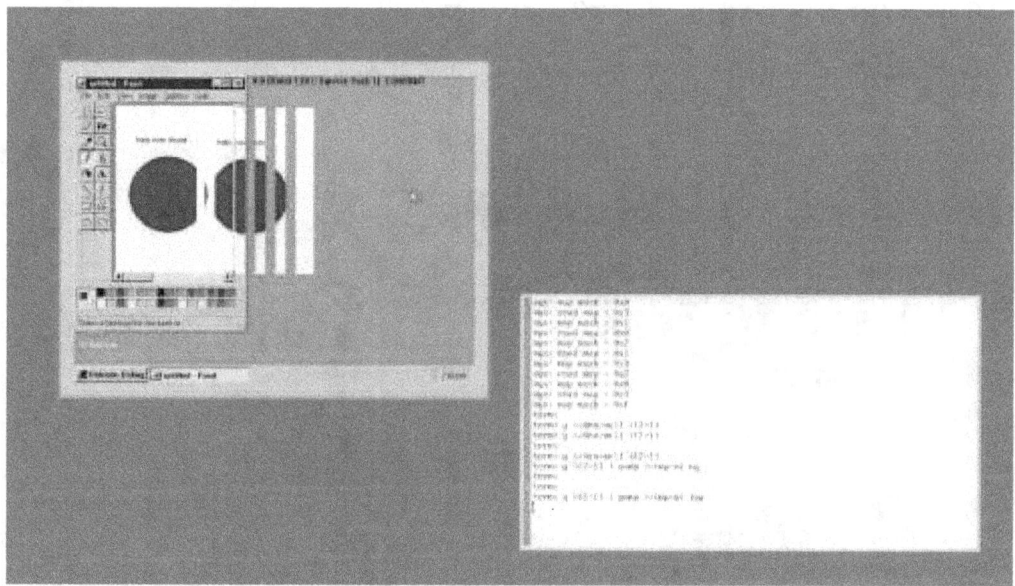

Classified.

8.8 – Additional Software

8.8.1 – 9front sources server

Additional 9front software is available from a 9P share that is accessible from any Plan 9 system:

```
9fs 9front
```

The following files and directories will then be available under `/n/`:

```
9front/ — 9front source
```

194

`9front.torrent` — torrent of current 9front ISO image

`extra/` — third party software source

`fqa/` — troff sources for 9front Frequently Questioned Answers

`hardware/` — known working hardware (sysinfo, firmware, manuals, etc.)

`iso/` — current 9front ISO image(s)

8.8.2 – 9front contrib

Some 9front users maintain a contrib directory on an official 9front 9P share (similar to the contrib arrangement provided by Bell Labs [now deprecated]) that is accessible from any Plan 9 system:

```
9fs 9contrib
```

User directories will then be available under `/n/contrib/`, and a mostly completete mirror of the defunct Bell Labs sources server will be available under `/n/sources/`.

These directories are also accessible via HTTP: `http://contrib.9front.org`

Note: The `contrib` directories are currently offline pending server reorganization.

8.8.3 – Other public 9p servers

A list of active public 9p servers is maintained here: `http://www.9paste.net/qrstuv/9pindex`

8.8.4 – Advanced Namespace Tools for Plan 9

ANTS is a collection of modifications and additional software which adds new namespace manipulation capabilities to Plan 9. It is free software based on 9front and uses the same licensing, MIT for original code, LPL for modifications of Bell Labs source. Download it here: `http://9gridchan.org`

8.8.5 – Even More Additional Software

```
> Anyways how about a list of software.

http://shithub.us/git/repos.html
https://github.com/henesy/awesome-plan9
https://sr.ht/projects?search=%23plan9
https://github.com/Plan9-Archive
https://github.com/topics/plan9
```

8.8.6 – Community Maintained Link For Additional Software

http://wiki.9front.org/extra

8.9 – Bootstrapping architectures not included on the ISO

8.9.1 – amd64

To setup the amd64 port, install the 386 port from the ISO, then cross compile and install the amd64 binaries and kernel. Or, simply install from the amd64 ISO.

Read: *FQA 5.2.2.1 – Cross compiling, FQA 7.2.5 – How do I install a new kernel?*

8.9.2 – Raspberry Pi

The most convenient way to use an rpi is to cross compile and install the arm binaries and the bcm kernel on the network file server, and then tcp boot the rpi.

Read: *FQA 5.2.2.1 – Cross compiling, FQA 6.7.1 – How do I tcp boot?*

Updated instructions for installing directly onto the rpi's sd card are detailed in *Appendix J – Junk*

8.9.3 – arm64

```
# create directory for arm64 files
mount -c /srv/boot /root
mkdir /root/arm64
cd /

# build arm64 compilers
for(i in /sys/src/cmd/7[acl]){cd $i && mk install}

# build remaining arm64 binaries
cd /sys/src
objtype=arm64
mk install
```

Read: *FQA 5.2.2.1 – Cross compiling, FQA 7.2.5 – How do I install a new kernel?*

8.10 – ACPI

Plan9front currently has partial ACPI support for PCI interrupt routing and system shut-down.

8.10.1 – Enabling ACPI

ACPI is now enabled by default. For machines without ACPI, disable it with the presence of *acpi=0 boot parameter.

The command aux/acpi presents at mountpoint (default /mnt/acpi) an interface to the ACPI. If a service is specified, the interface will be posted at /srv/service as well.

Read: acpi(8)

8.12 – Revision Control

8.12.1 – cvs

OpenCVS was ported to Plan 9.

Download it here: http://plan9.stanleylieber.com/src/cvs.tgz

An implementation of a cvs (client) file server, called cvsfs, was also created for Plan 9.

Download it here: http://plan9.stanleylieber.com/src/cvsfs.tgz

8.12.2 – git

There is a native `git` implementation availabe for plan 9. It has been added to the 9front distribution, but upstream is still located here: `http://shithub.us/ori/git9/HEAD/info.html`

Someone else wrote a shell script wrapper that attempts to replicate some basic `git` actions by downloading a zip file from the repository and performing operations on it.

Download it here: `http://plan9.stanleylieber.com/rc/git`

8.12.3 – Mercurial

9front ships with Mercurial.

Read: *FQA 5.2.1.1 – hgrc*

See also: `hgfs(4)`

8.12.4 – svn

No.

8.13 – Video

8.13.1 – treason

A video player for 9front. It can play H.264, AV1, VP8 and VP9-encoded MP4/MKV video files. Only 8-bit per component YUV 4:2:0 is supported atm.

Download it here: https://sr.ht/~ft/treason/

FQA 9 – Troubleshooting

9.1 – First

- STATE YOUR ASSUMPTIONS.

- `cat /etc/os-release` to verify you are not, in fact, running Ubuntu Linux with a Plan 9 theme.

- Are you running drawterm?

- Verify your OpenBSD configuration.

- Are you using the `qwerty` keyboard layout?

- Before reporting a bug, try the latest ISO image.

- MAKE SENSE.

- When all else fails, see: *FQA 2.4 – Reporting Bugs*

9.2 – Booting

9.2.1 – Boot parameters

- Immediately after the BIOS screen, hit any key until you see the > prompt. From there, values from `plan9.ini` may be temporarily added or changed. Read: `9boot(8)`

- Boot parameters beginning with a * are interpreted by the kernel. All other parameters are passed as enviroment variables to the boot process.

- Adding or changing a parameter: `param=value`

- Removing a parameter: `clear param=`

- When finished, type `boot` to resume booting.

9.2.2 – Break into a shell

At the `[bootargs]` prompt, type `!rc` and hit enter to break into a shell. Type `exit` to return to the `[bootargs]` prompt.

9.2.3 – Editing plan9.ini

• It is not possible to edit plan9.ini stored on the ISO, but parameters can be changed temporarily before booting. See above.

• On a harddrive installation, `plan9.ini` is stored with the bootloader and the kernel in a small FAT partition called 9fat at the beginning of the plan9 partition. The 9fat can be mounted by executing `9fs 9fat` from the livecd or the installed system. The file `/n/9fat/plan9.ini` can then be edited with a text editor like acme(1), sam(1) or ed(1).

• If your change to `plan9.ini` or the 9fat made the system unbootable, it is always possible to manually override parameters on the > prompt (see above) or start the system from the livecd and pick your installed cwfs or hjfs partition on the [bootargs] prompt. Example: `local!/dev/sdC0/fscache`

9.2.4 – Boot media not recognized

• Break into a shell, then type `grep   n '^01' '#$/pci/'*ctl` to get the pci vid/did of the installed disk controllers. then look in the sd drivers to see if the controller is already recognized.

• Sometimes, there is a problem with the drive, not the controller. `cat /dev/sd*/ctl` to get the status of the individual drives.

• Try different BIOS settings like AHCI/IDE mode.

• Try the USB troubleshooting steps (see below). Sometimes USB problems prevent unrelated devices from working properly.

9.2.5 – I moved my hard drive between ports

If your file system is cwfs(4):

• Let's assume it went from sdE0 to sdE1.

• At the bootargs prompt:

```
local!/dev/sdE1/fscache -c
filsys main c(/dev/sdE1/fscache)(/dev/sdE1/fsworm)
filsys dump o
filsys other /dev/sdE1/other
end
```

9.3 – Graphics

9.3.1 – Rio fails to start

See the discussion of graphics in *FQA 4 – 9front Installation Guide.* When you find a working mode, update your `plan9.ini`.

9.3.2 – VESA BIOS does not contain a valid mode

The standard solution is to have the customer send the computer back to the manufacturer, who reflashes the EEPROM with the correct information and return the computer to the customer.

9.4 – Networking

9.4.1 – Networking is not working

Read: *FQA 6.2.8 – Verifying network settings*

9.4.2 – Cannot resolve domain names

If `ndb/dns` is running but you are still unable to resolve domains, you can try adding a DNS server directly to `/net/ndb`.

Read: *FQA 6.2.5 – DNS Resolution*

9.4.3 – /mnt/web/clone does not exist

Programs that require `webfs(4)` to be running require `webfs(4)` to be running.

Read: `hget(1)`, `mothra(1)`

9.4.4 – PCMCIA WiFi stopped working after reboot

Do `fshalt` and power down completely instead of just rebooting with `fshalt -r`.

9.5 – USB

9.5.1 – Devices not recognized or not working

- Break into a shell, or simply type in a `rio` window: `cat /dev/usbevent` and try plugging in a USB device. If the devices where detected, some output should appear on screen. This doesnt mean we have a working driver for it but verifies that the USB controller and HUB driver recognized the device.

- Dump USB controller status to the console with echo dump >/dev/usb/ctl after that, you might recover the output from /dev/kmesg or run cat /dev/kprint in a separate rio window to not spill it all over the screen. Check the nintr and tdintr counters to see if they are all zero. If thats the case, then this is might be a interrupt routing problem sometimes caused by broken/incomplete BIOS MP tables. See below.

- If USB keyboard is the only option, try to enable PS2 emulation in the BIOS and disable kernel usb support. See below.

- if the machine employs a USB3.0 (xHCI) controller, try to disable USB3.0 support in BIOS as the driver may not support your chipset yet.

9.5.2 – System freezes after showing memory sizes

- The boot parameter *acpi=0 will disable ACPI (probably needed for 386 machines).

- Try the boot parameter *nomp= to disable multiprocessor mode.

- Try the boot parameter *nousbehci= (This disables USB 2.0.)

- Try the boot parameter *nousbuhci=

- Try the boot parameter *nousbohci=

- Try the boot parameter *nousbprobe= (This disables USB completely)

9.6 – auth This space left intentionally blank.

9.999999999999999999999999999999999999999 – GIVE UP

Give up now.

Go away.

Every joke is a tiny revolution
— George Orwell

Appendix B – Bounties

INTRODUCTION

This is a wish list that has evolved over time to money.

PLEDGE

Pledge a bounty for a specific task by writing a message to the 9front mailing list. Say what you mean, offer a definite price, and be prepared to pay up when someone fulfills your request, deadbeat.

PENDING

Searchable PDFs in page *$200*
"look" command that allows me to search for text in PDFs

3D Accelerated Graphics *$1*
what

fully functional, read/write hgfs *$55*
Why should we need python and mercurial just to work with mercurial repositories?

fully functional, read/write gitfs *$5*
Why should anyone port git to Plan 9?

ICC color profiles *$10*
Support for calibrating displays using custom ICC color profiles. This is most useful for making livable laptops that have shitty LCD panels.

MP4/VP9 video support *$200*
Decoder and/or encoder. Details to be determined. Some work in this area was done by mischief and he was paid $200 of the original $400 bounty. Sigrid has take this a lot farther, displaying youtube videos in full motion.

vcardfs *$5*
File system for vCard files, preferably read AND write. sl will actually pay for this.

USB WiFi driver (you choose hardware) *$5*
sl's ThinkPad X1 Tablet 1st Gen still can't WiFi.

SSH server *$5*
SSH straight to 9front and authenticate with 9front user credentials. Potential use cases include: SSH from phones, serve git, etc.

fix/polish hubfs, or create TMUX-alike *$5*
When you SSH in from a phone, you don't want to do a lot of typing to resume where you left off before your network connection dropped. kvik may qualify for this prize with pin(1).

dmenu-bar for the i3-like rio replacement with useful info *30 euros*
Some info that should be possible to display: workspaces, system info (cpu load, memory load, network load, ...), digital 24h clock. If not configurable, the bar should be at the top of the screen on all work spaces.

configuration-file based customization of the i3-like rio replacement and dmenu-like bar *20 euros*
A configuration file where key bindings and colours can be adjusted.

games/md Sega CD support *$5*
SNATCHER wasn't a cartridge game.

games/tg16 TurboGrafx 16 *$5*
Should exist.

OneDrive file system *20€*
Must Have (20€)

* File management (full CRUD support). * Works with OneDrive. * Works with Sharepoint Drives. * Works with official Microsoft servers (office.com stuff).

Should Have

* User keys in factotum. * No complicated configuration. Auth info, drive (and maybe server?) should be enough. * Native C preferred (9front).

Nice to Have (+5€)

* Access versions: File versions are provided by OneDrive/Sharepoint. Use these. * Lazy caching: OneDrive protocol provides sha1sums. Files could be stored in a persistent cache (simple directory?). cat file >/dev/null& for manually caching is fine. * some way to show files are cached (maybe with ls?).

arm64 golang + gofmt *$500*

I will also accept simply being able to run GOOS=plan9 GOARCH=amd on the 64-bit plan9 pi image.

DONE (pay up, deadbeats)

Intel 8260 WiFi driver *$5*
sl's ThinkPad X1 Tablet 1st Gen can't WiFi. DONE (pay cinap)

dwm/i3/sway-like rio replacement *50 euros*
10 work spaces, tiling, start terminal with $mod+enter, switch work space with $mod+number. DONE (paid sigrid)

Native Intel VGA Driver *$260*
People want to be able to access resolutions not presented via VESA. DONE (pay cinap)

Bookmark Support in page(1) *$10*
People want to bookmark things in PDFs and such, to come back to later. (How about generic "snarf where I am" support? Some want to copy image path/name.) DONE (pay cinap)

Quake *$5*
Apparently Doom is not good enough. DONE (pay qwx)

bsdemu *$1*
Linuxemu is the Linux treadmill. Since the point of all this is being able to run software not supported in Plan 9, rather than simply worshipping Linux, OpenBSD makes more sense as a base platform, since the contents of its ports tree are both 1.) (now) reasonably up to date, and 2.) to some extent, pre-checked for abrigations of sanity. Syscalls are still out of control, but let's examine the real cost/benefit of the emulation approach. DONE (see vmx(1)) (pay aiju)

look *$5*
put the look command in rio DONE (pay cinap)

fix webfs to work with livejournal.com *$1*
Currently, after logging in to livejournal.com, webfs gets stuck in a 302 redirect loop when visiting any account_name.livejournal.com virtual host. DONE (pay cinap)

replace p9sk1 with something better *$10*
We're sitting ducks. DONE (pay cinap)

qemu or qemu-alike *$50*
PC hardware virtualization. Expose guest resources to the host. Forget about linuxemu/bsdemu forever. DONE (see vmx(1)) (pay aiju)

improve TLS support *$10*
The tls(3) device implements the record layer protocols of Transport Layer Security version 1.0 and Secure Sockets Layer version 3.0. It does not implement the handshake protocols, which are responsible for mutual authentication and key exchange. 9fans has debated what form expansion of TLS should take. Wanted: more ciphers, support for user certificates, support for certificate verification. ECDSA! ECDHE! Also: SNI support in tlssrv.

Some work has already been done:

libsec: implement tlsClient support for RFC6066 server name identification (SNI) (pay cinap)

libsec: add TLS_DHE_RSA_WITH_3DES_EDE_CBC_SHA client cipher suit support (pay cinap)

libsec: add aes_128_cbc and aes_256_cbc ciphers (pay mischief)

libsec/x509: use SHA2-256 digest algorithm instead of MD5 (pay cinap)

libsec/tlshand: implement client side ECDHE (pay pr)

libsec: TLS1.1 support (needs new devtls) (pay cinap)

libsec: TLS1.2 client support (pay cinap)

libsec: TLS1.2 server support, make cipher list with most prefered first (pay cinap)

libsec: add TLS_RSA_WITH_AES_128_CBC_SHA256 and TLS_RSA_WITH_AES_256_CBC_SHA256 ciphers (pay mischief)

libsec: add curve25519() from http://code.google.com/p/curve25519-donna/ (pay cinap)

libsec: add rfc5869 hmac-based key derivation function hkdf_x() (pay cinap)

libsec: add TLS_ECDHE_ECDSA_WITH_AES_128_CBC_SHA256 and TLS_ECDHE_RSA_WITH_AES_128_CBC_SHA256 cipher suits (pay cinap)

libsec: implement client certificate authentication for tls1.2 (pay cinap)

libsec: add poly1305 (pay cinap)

libsec: add chacha cipher (from charles forsyth) (pay cinap)

libsec: add chacha20 poly1305 aead, allow 64 bit iv's for chacha, add tsmemcmp() (pay cinap)

tls: implement chacha20/poly1305 aead cipher suits (pay cinap)

libsec: add salsa20 stream cipher (pay cinap)

libsec: ecdsa client support for tlshand (pay cinap)

libsec: add libc.h include for aes_xts.c (drawterm) (pay cinap)

libsec: implement elliptic curve group operations in jacobian coordinate system (pay cinap)

libsec: implement server side SCSV preventing silly client fallbacks (pay cinap)

shit ton of other tls work (pay cinap)

Appendix G – GSOC

GSOC project ideas

Difficulty on a scale 1–5

Generally all of our projects require C programming and prior experience with C is a prerequisite for all of them. Prior experience with Plan 9, while not technically a prerequisite, is extremely helpful and any student is advised to at least carefully read the Plan 9 documentation before applying.

MPEG–4 decoder (4)

The goal of this project is to create a video decoder to allow native playback of MPEG–4 video. This is a very challenging project that requires a very solid background in C. Potential mentors: cinap_lenrek Skills: Reading and understanding the MPEG–4 documentation which probably requires a certain minimum of mathematical skills, writing and debugging complex programs

Sam scrolling and other GUI work (2)

Scrolling in the text editor sam is currently very erratic. The goal of this project is to improve on this situation. This project does not require much programming per se but it does require analyzing, understanding and improving existing code. This project would probably be extended to fixing other GUI problems. Potential mentors: cinap_lenrek, Ori_B Skills: being able to innovate, coming up with algorithms for GUI problems such as scrolling

Improved APE (2)

Our ANSI/POSIX emulation layer is currently very unpolished and improving the coverage would be a worthwhile project. This is not very difficult but probably a lot of work. Potential mentors: cinap_lenrek, Ori_B Skills: reading ANSI/POSIX documentation, debugging code written by other people

Drivers (3)

This project would consist of multiple drivers (to be decided) that need to be written. This project is modestly challenging. Potential mentors: cinap_lenrek Skills: general systems programming, prior OS development experience helpful

DjVu/CHM/Jbig2 support (2)

Our document reader page(1) needs DjVu, CHM and Jbig2 (PDF encoding) support. Another project that's not particularly challenging but a lot of work. Potential mentors: cinap_lenrek, Ori_B Skills: reading and implementing documentation for various document standards, some experience with image processing probably helpful

Improving acid (3)

Our debugger acid(1) lacks several useful debugging features that might be worth looking into, such as watchpoints. The goal would be to research what might be good features and implement them. This may require kernel changes. Potential mentors: cinap_lenrek Skills: general systems programming, familiarity with low-level concepts

Implement ECDSA and ECDHE for TLS (2)

This would be implementing the ECC cipher suits for TLS (rfc4492) with libsecs ec(2) functions. This should be a relatively easy task for beginners. Potential mentors: cinap_lenrek Skills: reading standards, reading code, cryptopgraphy

Version control hosting support for werc (1)

Werc is a web anti-framework written in rc, the Plan 9 shell. rc-httpd is an HTTP server written in the same language. 9front uses git for version control -- but nobody's done much work on making 9front able to *host* git repos. This project would involve setting up werc and rc-httpd on a 9front System, then teaching werc to work with hg to host repositories. For bonus points, test your changes on a UNIX system to make sure it's portable! Potential mentors: khm Skills: web stuff, mercurial, rc scripting **Note:** 9front has recently switched from mercurial hosted on 9front to git hosted on 9front, so this project may now be obsolete. (Pending redaction.)

Internet of things project: use 9p for sensor networks (1-2)

Write a 9p server and client (as you see fit) on the orchestrator and nodes. Create and evaluate text-based protocol for 9p-based sensor network orchestration. You can use rpi for everything, but are also free to choose a low-power solution for the nodes if you're up for some low-level C programming experience. Potential mentors: jpm Skills: soldering, theory of sensor networks, C

Appendix J – Junk

Raspberry Pi

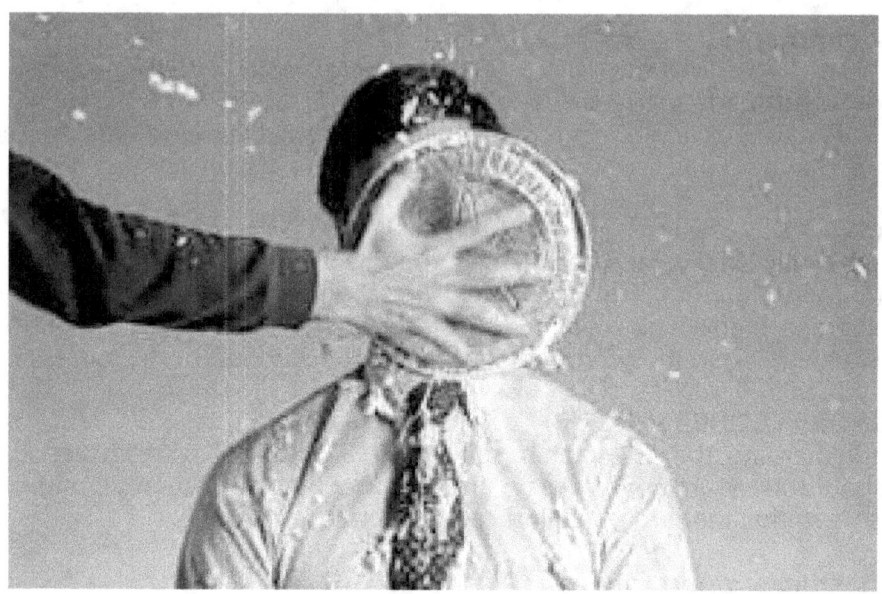

Installation Instructions

The last release introduces support for raspi1,2 and 3 and you can build a sdcard image that will be bootable on raspi by running:

```
# build arm userspace
cd /sys/src
objtype=arm
mk install

# download raspi firmware
cd /sys/src/boot/bcm
mk

# build 32 bit arm kernel for raspi (pi2 also works for raspi3)
cd /sys/src/9/bcm
mk 'CONF=pi' install
mk 'CONF=pi2' install

# build bootable hjfs sdcard image for raspi
cd /sys/lib/dist
bind / /n/src9
mk /path/to/somethingsomething.pi.img
```

Once booted on the Raspberry Pi, you're able to mount the dos partition with:

```
9fs pidos
```

This will mount the dos partition on /n/pidos, similar to how 9fs 9fat works.

C

Read: *Plan 9 C Compilers, How to Use the Plan 9 C Compiler*

C++

Read: *Bjarne Stroustrup: "I Did It For You All..."*

C#

Go

Note: The following instructions may be more up to date: `http://wiki.9front.org/building-go`

For now, this still works:

```
# automatically converted ca certs from mozilla.org
hget https://curl.haxx.se/ca/cacert.pem >/sys/lib/tls/ca.pem

# shell script that emulates git commands
hget http://9front.org/extra/rc/git >$home/bin/rc/git
chmod 775 $home/bin/rc/git

# fetch the repository
git clone https://go.googlesource.com/go
cd go
git checkout go1.4.2     # amd64 only: bootstrap with 1.4.2

# build go
cd src
./make.rc

# install documentation
go get golang.org/x/tools/cmd/godoc

# go!
```

Read: *Documentation – The Go Programming Language* and *Go Plan 9 Wiki*

Haskell

Perl

Perl 5.8.0, ported to Plan 9: http://plan9.bell–labs.com/sources/extra/perl.iso.bz2

PHP

Python

Python 2.5.1 is included with the 9front distribution, not because anyone loves Python, but because it was required by Mercurial (also loved by no one), which was required by Google Code (shutting down in 2015). An abject lesson in expediency.

Jeff Sickel ported Python 2.7 to Plan 9.

Ruby

Read: *Ruby is Not Even Funny*

I am now used to the FQA being frankly not worth the 1s and 0s it was written in
— 웃e 웃 웃☺r웃

Once upon a time, khm was searching for `rails documentation` and accidentally hit the `Images` link. In the first page of results was a photo of the train tracks of Auschwitz. Its presence among the Ruby on Rails logos was so absurd and out of place that khm memorialized it. It was made in an era before actual Nazis had re-entered the public dialogue, so it felt like Google Image Search was denigrating Ruby on Rails by including this sort of imagery in the results.

Generally speaking, 4chan types read it as an endorsement, which sucks. More recently, people who are not assholes have also begun to read it as an endorsement, which is even more unfortunate. Finally, the people who just get mad about things on social media have begun nesting in it. As a result, this image has been targeted for redaction by the 9front Internet Mob Mollification committee.

Read: `https://news.ycombinator.com/item?id=25777580`,

`https://mastodon.social/@stevelord/105509463981426031`,

`https://lobste.rs/s/2tvtwp`

FQA Appendix T – TODO

Introduction

This is a list of possible things to add, remove, change in 9front. After there's been some consensus that something here is going to be implemented, an issue may be created on the bug tracker (which no longer exists).

Crazy Ideas

- make a TODO list which isn't full of bullshit and random suggestions

Basically Sound

- dan cross' sor
  http://permalink.gmane.org/gmane.os.plan9.general/8755

- video decoder/player (ffmpeg port?) (see *FQA Appendix B – Bounties*)

- graphviz

- equis:

    → use /dev/kbd (for video game emulators, amongst other things)

    → snarf/paste support (might be good as client program—how would this work?)

- openvpn

- unrar 3

- un7zip

- VacFS

- client auth

- groups (?)

- write access

- N64, PSX, SMS, TG-16 emulators

- music tracker program (sequencer), see: sigrid's native FastTracker II clone

- pico(1) (the plan 9 image manipulation language), see: `http://nopenopenope.net/posts/pico`

- OPUS audio support
`http://tools.ietf.org/html/rfc6716`

- djvu support

- chm support
`http://www.nongnu.org/chmspec/latest/index.html`

- GUI programs (mothra, abaco, sam, etc.) should have shift+up/down arrow behavior like rio

- add magnet/dht and peer discovery support to ip/torrent

- implement some way to determine used and free space on FAT volumes

Somebody Else's Problem
- inferno:

  → make snarf work by default

  → fix build on amd64

For the Masochists
- write NTFS driver

- exfat filesystem

For the Users
- read fqa

- read man pages

- read plan 9 papers

- learn c

FQA Appendix Z – Getting Started With 9front

Many users are not only new to 9front, but new to Plan 9.

You may be lost.

Read: http://massivefictions.com/NO_COMPUTER/

Listen: https://archive.org/download/Piracy/Piracy-Track_04-Nobody_Listens_vbr.mp3

Self-test: http://n-gate.com

NOTES